THE TRIAL OF JOB

HEAVEN'S COURTROOM, THE HUMAN SOUL, AND RIGHTEOUS SUFFERING

THE TRIAL OF
JOB

*HEAVEN'S COURTROOM, THE HUMAN
SOUL, AND RIGHTEOUS SUFFERING*

TABITHA MIN

RITTER HOUSE
PUBLISHING

Scripture quotations taken from the Modern English Version, copyright © 2014 by Military Bible Association Inc. Used by permission of Passio/Charisma Media. All rights reserved.
Unless otherwise indicated, all Scripture quotations are from the Modern English Version (MEV).

The Ritter House Publishing name and logo are trademarks of Ritter House Publishing LLC.

www.tabithamin.com
Book and Cover design by Tabitha Min

ISBN: 979-8-9937889-1-3
First Edition: December 2025
10 9 8 7 6 5 4 3 2 1

This book is dedicated to the women of our Bible study, whose courage to wrestle honestly with Scripture and suffering created the soil from which this work grew. And to those who find this book unexpectedly, may it meet you gently where you are.

And to my husband, whose support, faithfulness, and encouragement have accompanied this work since its earliest beginnings. Thank you for your presence, then and now.

TABLE OF CONTENTS

PREFACE

Many questions remain unresolved throughout the Bible, and truthfully speaking, I wrestled for a long time with not having the answers. The book of Job is well known for leaving its readers with unresolved tension in many ways. In the past, I feared having to face such mystery and tension, but now I find that mystery most worthy of my worship.

For a time, I believed that worshiping the Lord required approaching Him with a certain level of decorum and reverence when I came before the throne of grace. And while such reverence is good, I misunderstood the invitation. One can absolutely stand in awe and worship the Lord from a distance, just as the Israelites trembled at the power of the One who rested on the mountain. He is indeed a very powerful and very dangerous God. His voice alone can level the mountains and shatter the cedars of Lebanon. Yet He is also the One who speaks life and peace alongside the stillness of His love.

For many years, I stood at the base of the mountain, worshiping the Lord from a distance for fear that His holiness might consume me. But what He has taught me through His patience and love is that such worship lacked the very intimacy I so desperately craved. And like Moses,

He is calling each of us to enter the storm itself, so that we may find the stillness of His heart at the center.

And so, the question remains whether or not we can trust Him enough to enter that storm at all. What He desires with us—just as He has since the beginning of creation—is to bridge the chasm that stands between us and grant us the kind of intimacy He has always intended.

Job is a testament to that very dilemma. And it is through his story that we may find answers to our own longing and desire for intimacy with the One who calls to us from the whirlwind.

INTRODUCTION

This book, quite simply, did not begin as a companion.

For the past two years, I have been studying the book of Job and slowly collecting notes as I have tried to understand its structure, themes, and the kind of questions the book itself is asking. So, when our Bible study decided together that we would be spending time in Job, I realized that many of those notes could be gathered into a single place and offered as a companion to the study itself.

Originally, this material was meant to become something much larger. But given the depth and complexity of Job—and the reality of walking through it week by week—I chose instead to compile a condensed version that focuses on the larger framework of the text. This book is intended to help readers recognize the layers within Job and the themes that connect them, so that the weekly study can remain grounded and coherent rather than fragmented.

This book is not meant to replace the study, nor is it required reading. It exists simply as a reference for those who want additional context as we move through the text together.

It is also important to say clearly what this book is not.

This is not a scholarly commentary, and it is not intended to function as a definitive or argumentative interpretation of the book of Job. I am not a scholar or a theologian. I am simply a fellow teacher in a women's Bible study sharing what I have come to understand through my own study, prayer, and engagement with the text. What you will find here reflects my personal reading of Job as I have wrestled with it over time. This book does not rely on or quote any single modern source or commentary.

And most importantly, the book of Job raises questions that do not resolve easily. It confronts suffering, justice, silence, and faith in ways that resist simple answers. Life itself often forces us into those same questions, and Job gives language to that experience. Because of this, I would encourage readers to move through both this book and the study slowly, with patience and grace for their own process.

This companion is meant to support that journey. So if it helps you see the structure of Job more clearly, recognize recurring themes, or approach the text with greater depth and attentiveness, then it has done what it was intended to do. And if it prompts further questions rather than final answers, that, too, is consistent with the nature of the book itself.

My hope is that this book encourages you and draws you into a deeper, more intimate relationship with our Creator.

BEFORE YOU BEGIN

This book serves as a companion to a weekly study on the book of Job, where many of these themes are explored further through discussion and teaching. If you'd like to follow along or go deeper, the full series is available as a podcast teaching.

Scan the QR code below to listen on **Spotify**, or find the teachings on **YouTube** at: **@HiddenThreadChannel**

CHAPTER ONE

The Complexity of Job

It is widely agreed that the book of Job is one of the most complex books in Scripture. Many people find themselves confused by it, and others simply avoid it or skim through it because the story seems to turn unexpectedly or appear contradictory in places.

Job uniquely pushes against our instinctual way of reading the Bible. It challenges our theology, demands a kind of philosophical patience, and operates within an ancient worldview that most modern readers are no longer familiar with.

Because of this, when people read or teach Job, they often fall back on the safest, most familiar responses like, "When life is hard, trust God." "Suffering shapes you." "We don't always understand why things happen." And while these statements aren't wrong, they tend to remain on the surface of the text.

But the very complexity that makes Job difficult is also the thing that invites us into it. Job is asking the reader to step into the tension—to sit with the questions and wrestle with them—just as Job wrestles in real time with God, with his friends, and with the turmoil of his own soul.

Why Most Modern Christians Misread Job

When most readers approach the book, we instinctively frame it around a single question: "Why do good people suffer?" It feels like the natural entry point because suffering is the first thing we encounter in Job's story, and it is often the first thing we want resolved in our own lives. We read Job through the lens of our own pain, our own fear, and our own longing for answers. So naturally, suffering becomes the focus.

But the book itself is not asking that question.

In fact, the narrative goes out of its way to show us that Job is not suffering because he has done anything wrong. It tells us this at the outset so that we won't get stuck in that line of reasoning. And yet, we still return to it, trying to make Job's pain fit neatly into an explanation we can understand.

If we read Job primarily as a book about human suffering, we will inevitably miss the larger narrative shaping the entire story. But if we read Job as a book about the righteousness of God, then the chaos, the silence, the arguments, the poetry, and even the restoration begin to take on a deeper and richer meaning. The central question then shifts away from, "Why is Job suffering?" and toward, "What is God revealing about Himself through Job?"

This, in my opinion, is the true doorway into the book. And once you step through it, the entire story opens itself in a way that is altogether layered, intentional, and wonderfully profound.

CHAPTER ONE

An Ancient Interpretation

The idea that Job is a Christ-centered book is not new by any means. And what I am presenting here isn't something novel or unconventional. Many early church fathers like Origen, Gregory the Great, Irenaeus, and Chrysostom approached Job with extraordinary theological depth, consistently recognizing Christ woven throughout its pages.

They saw Job as a prophetic shadow of the Man of Sorrows, and a righteous sufferer whose innocence pointed forward to Jesus. They understood Job's cry for a Mediator as more than personal agony, and a glimpse into humanity's deepest need. They read Job as a cosmic argument about the righteousness of God, and far more than a meditation on suffering or a collection of moral lessons. Their focus was on perceiving the larger story God was telling.

Today, most of us approach Scripture from a different starting point, not out of neglect or disinterest, but because the questions we bring to the Bible have changed over time. Modern readers often look for guidance, encouragement, stability, or help navigating the emotional turbulence of life. These are sincere needs, and God absolutely meets us there. But that approach often causes books like Job to be filtered through a therapeutic lens, where it becomes primarily about surviving hardship or trusting God when life doesn't make sense.

Those themes are present, of course, but they are not the foundation of the narrative. And when we read Job in this light, we can unintentionally overlook the deeper theological framework that holds the story together.

Yet this shift is not a disadvantage; it's an invitation. Because now we have the opportunity to rediscover the mysteries of Scripture through stories like Job in ways that feel both fresh and unexpectedly powerful.

We can step back into the ancient world with new eyes, allowing the text to speak at the depth it was written, and in doing so, rediscover treasures that earlier generations saw clearly but we have nearly forgotten.

Job as the Bridge of the Entire Canon

Job also holds a strange and beautiful place in Scripture. It is one of the earliest books ever written, as some scholars believe it predates much of the Pentateuch, yet it sits near the center of our Bibles. This placement seems far from accidental as Job acts as a kind of center of gravity, and a bridge that ties the entire story of redemption together.

In this way, Job becomes more than a story of ancient suffering, but one that becomes a narrative reaching backward to the origins of humanity as it stretches forward into the fullness of Christ.

Job echoes backward to Eden, not only because it begins with a righteous man in perfect harmony with God's blessing, but because a heavenly accuser reappears with the same familiar challenge: "Is God truly good?" and "Are His motives trustworthy?" Eden is the birthplace of that question, and Job becomes the proving ground where it is confronted again.

At the same time, Job anticipates forward to the Cross. His cry for a Mediator, his innocence in the face of suffering, and his anguish that is met with silence all foreshadows the One who would become the true Righteous Sufferer. Job sits in ashes, longing for someone to stand between God and man. Then Jesus steps into the world to become exactly that.

And the book also shadows the heavenly courtroom revealed in Revelation. John's vision in Revelation 12, where the accuser stands before God day and night, mirrors the cosmic courtroom scene that opens Job's story. Therefore, the conflict in Job is not random or isolated; it is part of the larger spiritual drama Scripture unfolds from Genesis to Revelation.

This is why Jesus' words matter so deeply in which He says, "All Scripture testifies of Me" (John 5:39).

If that is true—and Jesus says it is—then Job is not merely a detour or a theological curiosity. Job is a witness, and is part of that very testimony.

It makes perfect sense, then, that a book written so early, placed so centrally, and framed around the cosmic question of God's righteousness would serve as a bridge across the entire canon. From Eden to Calvary, and from the heavenly courtroom to the final victory of Christ, the story of Job stands right in the middle, quietly holding the threads together.

Why Job Matters Now

We are living in a time where many believers feel the ground shifting beneath them. People are hungry for depth in a way previous generations may not have articulated. There is a growing sense that shallow teaching doesn't hold up under the weight of real life, and that the easy answers we once leaned on simply cannot sustain us through seasons of true suffering. At the same time, many Christians feel spiritually isolated; caught between their longing for God and the silence that seems to meet them in their darkest moments. Add to this the increasing visibility of suffering in our world, and the growing rediscovery of the supernatural worldview of Scripture, and it becomes clear that Job speaks into our moment with an almost prophetic relevance.

But Job doesn't offer quick fixes or tidy formulas. Instead, it confronts us with the nature of God: His righteousness, His sovereignty, His mystery, and His nearness. It exposes the limits of cliché and challenges the instinct to reduce God to something manageable or predictable. The book forces us to reckon with the architecture of the human soul through our fears, our longing, our inner contradictions, and our deep ache for the God who sometimes seems hidden.

And woven through all of this is a reminder of our desperate need for a Mediator. Job feels that need in the marrow of his suffering long before the incarnation, and his cry becomes a kind of doorway into the gospel. His longing tells the truth about us, in that we cannot stand before God on our own. We were made for Someone who can bridge that infinite gap.

Job also has something powerful to say about suffering itself. It does not treat suffering as punishment, nor as a mysterious cosmic accident. Instead, it reveals suffering as the place where sanctification works at its deepest level. In Job's story, suffering becomes the crucible where intimacy with God is refined, where false beliefs fall away, and where the soul is stripped down until all that remains is the raw and honest cry for the living God.

Job models that honesty for us with a unique kind of clarity. He doesn't hide his anguish, and he doesn't pretend to be unshaken. Instead, he brings every contradictory emotion directly to God, and in doing so, he reveals a kind of intimacy that most of us rarely see or practice. The book shows us that intimacy with God is not forged in comfort, but in the ashes, where all pretenses collapse and all we have left to offer Him is our unvarnished heart.

And then, at the end of it all, the story reveals a God who steps into the whirlwind. A God who answers, not by explaining Himself, but by revealing Himself. A God who vindicates Job's faith, and in doing so, vindicates His own righteousness before heaven and earth.

This is why Job matters now.

It is not a book about how to survive trials. It is a book about the mystery of God, His righteousness, and the kind of intimacy that is born when everything else is stripped away.

In a world that is desperate for shallow comfort but starving for real truth, Job offers us something far better: a God who meets us in the whirlwind and a faith that is strong enough to wrestle with Him there.

NOTES

NOTES

CHAPTER TWO

Literary Structure

One of the first things to notice when reading Job is that the book does not speak in a single voice. Job is intentionally built on a dual framework, with two literary worlds woven together to reveal two very different ways of seeing reality by which structure itself is part of the message. In fact, without paying attention to this design, the book's meaning is very easy to miss.

The opening and closing chapters (1–2 and 42:7–17) are written in prose: a straightforward narrative that reads like a historical report. It is calm, orderly, and seemingly straight forward. But this prose does far more than tell us a story. It lifts the curtain on the spiritual realm and places the reader directly inside the divine council setting.

We see what Job never sees. We witness conversations Job is never told about. We hear accusations he never knows were made. And we learn from the very beginning that his suffering is not random, not punitive, and not a result of moral failure. We are anchored in a larger heavenly reality that transcends Job's earthly experience.

The prose then functions as the macro lens perspective which is looking from heaven to earth. It frames the entire book as a type of courtroom scene. This narrative lens thus pulls the reader upward, urging us to watch the story unfold from above rather than from within the chaos.

Then, without warning, the book shifts. At the start of chapter 3, the narrative drops away and we fall headlong into poetry. And it's not gentle or lyrical poetry; this is the raw and emotionally charged language of the soul under pressure. From chapter 3 all the way to 42:6, the story unfolds almost entirely in poetic form. This is deliberate. Poetry, in this sense, is the only language capable of carrying the emotional weight of Job's experience.

So, where the prose gives us the courtroom of heaven, the poetry gives us the landscape of Job's heart. It exposes his grief, his outrage, his longing, his confusion, and his relentless pursuit of God. It mirrors the structure of ancient courtroom hymns, lament psalms, and wisdom dialogues—genres designed to give shape to the inner wrestling of humanity when answers never seem to come.

Poetry is where theology and emotion collide. It is where doctrine stretches, where human reason bends, and where intimacy with God is tested in the throes of silence. This middle section pulls us down into the dust beside Job, allowing us to feel his bewilderment and hear the tremble in his voice as he navigates the storm of his own psyche.

Prose, then, is the voice of heaven's perspective. And poetry is the voice of human experience. The genius of Job, however, is that both voices speak at the same time.

Job is one story told in two languages:

- the language of heaven

- and the language of the human soul

Two worlds are moving in tandem until the final collision meets in the whirlwind, where God's voice breaks through the storm and reunites the split perspectives into a single revelation. This is what makes Job one of the most psychologically and theologically richest works in all of Scripture.

Why the Middle is Poetry

When we leave the ordered narrative of chapters 1–2 and enter chapter 3, the language itself changes. And this shift is not accidental, it is the only way to faithfully convey the internal world Job is being pushed into.

Hebrew poetry is not built on rhyme or meter. It breathes in parallelism. This form mirrors the emotional and spiritual reality Job is actively experiencing. Parallelism allows the text to hold tension, contradiction, and layered truth all at once. It is the ideal structure for what Job is walking through, because his soul is not tidy, his thoughts are not linear, and his grief does not follow a straight line.

Thus, poetry allows space for what prose cannot hold.

The middle of Job is written in poetry because Job's soul is in crisis. And when the soul is unraveling, language begins to unravel with it. The prose of the opening chapters speaks with clarity because heaven sees clearly. But the poetry of the middle speaks with tremor and fragmentation because humanity does not.

The reader must feel the disorientation Job feels. And the reader must experience the stretch between what heaven knows and what Job perceives. So, the reader must enter the ache, and not simply observe it. Prose would flatten that ache, but poetry gives it room to breathe.

Thus, poetry becomes the only way to express what cannot be explained. When Job curses the day of his birth, when he argues with his friends, and when he pleads for God to answer, the emotional intensity refuses to be compressed into narrative simplicity. These are not moments for clean sentences and tidy explanations. They are moments of existential unraveling, where grief and faith collide in a kind of raw and trembling honesty.

So, the structure of the book itself becomes part of the message.

The beginning and end are prose because they give us heaven's perspective in which it is ordered, objective, and unshaken by circumstance. While the entire middle is poetry because it gives us the interior world of a man trying to reconcile his faith with the silence of God.

So, the text does not merely tell you what Job felt, it pulls you into his emotional storm. Then it asks you to stand in the tension with him.

In this way, the dual structure becomes a kind of spiritual formation for the reader. By the time you emerge from the poetic section and return to prose in chapter 42, you are not the same person who began the journey. The book has forced you to live inside Job's psyche long enough to understand that the questions he asks are not merely philosophical, they are the cries of covenant intimacy.

So, poetry becomes the language of the soul speaking to God in the dark. And this places the reader in a unique role as someone who knows more than Job, yet must walk beside him through the darkness without resolving it prematurely.

The narrative invites us to rise into the clarity of heaven's viewpoint, but it never lets us escape the ache of the human one. We are held, sometimes uncomfortably, between the truth of what God knows and what Job experiences. And it is in that very stretch that wisdom is cultivated.

Because if the reader refuses to ascend to heaven's perspective, the entire book collapses into confusion. Interpreted purely from the dust of earth, Job becomes a tangled mess of contradictions through undeserved suffering, unanswered questions, misguided friends, and a God who appears silent for far too long. This is why so many readers walk away unsure of what they just encountered. They remain trapped inside the earth-problem lens, reading Job as if it were merely a psychological drama or a study in perseverance. Without the heavenly vantage point, the story feels incomplete, and even chaotic.

But Job is not written to be understood from earth alone. It is written as a living tension between two ways of knowing. Yet, these are not competing narratives, they are complementary revelations. The prose establishes the unshakable truth of God's righteousness, while the poetry exposes the fragility of human perception beneath the weight of suffering. And the book asks the reader to hold both at once. Not because one negates the other, but because together they form the full shape of what it means to walk with God in a world where heaven is hidden and the soul is laid bare.

This is the tension of intimacy.

True communion with God requires us to trust what we cannot see while being honest about what we actually feel. Job teaches us that intimacy with God is not forged by choosing heaven's truth over our human anguish, nor by drowning truth beneath emotion, but by allowing the two to stand side by side until the voice in the whirlwind draws them into unity.

How Modern Readers Misread Job

It should come as no surprise, then, that modern readers often misread Job, not because the book is unclear, but because we instinctively read it from the wrong vantage point. Like we discussed earlier, most people never leave the earthly perspective, so the entire narrative feels distorted. When the lens stays fixed on earth, the book can only be understood at the level of human pain, and everything else becomes flattened or misunderstood. So, most readers approach Job assuming a handful of familiar expectations.

They see Job as a book about suffering, as if the story exists primarily to offer comfort in hardship or to explain why bad things happen. They see the friends as bad theologians, and caricatures of what not to say to someone in pain. They see Job as whining, speaking too freely or too emotionally. They see God's answer as "not answering," as though the whirlwind were a divine deflection instead of a revelation. And they see the ending as problematic prosperity, an uncomfortable return to blessing that seems to undermine everything the story wrestled with.

Why does this happen?

Because the reader never leaves the earthly perspective. They assume that Job is the point, that Job's pain is the center, and that Job's questions are the theme. But when we read the book this way, everything collapses into sentiment and confusion. I believe that the story was never meant to be interpreted solely from the ground. Rather, the author seems to be doing something far more complex.

Job's faith becomes evidence in a cosmic lawsuit. The adversary challenges God's claim about humanity. And Job becomes the battleground for the most ancient question of all that asks, *Is God good?*

The poetry becomes the sound of a soul grappling with God's silence. And the prose quietly reveals the meaning the characters themselves can never see. What looks like disconnected pieces from the earthbound perspective becomes a unified argument when viewed from above.

So, the book is not simply a narrative; it is a literary masterpiece of duality.

The poetic middle, therefore, is not about Job's suffering in isolation. It immerses the reader into Job's relationship with God through his intimacy, his honest struggle, and his refusal to let go of the One who seems hidden. And it is astonishing how often modern studies reduce this rich tapestry into the simple question of *why do bad things happen to good people?* But the book never asks that question. The deeper questions— the ones actually embedded in the narrative—are these:

Can love for God exist without reward?

What does covenant intimacy sound like when stripped bare?

The poetry forces the reader not to analyze these questions from a safe distance but to feel them. It draws the reader into confusion, longing, and despair intertwined with faith. It presses upon the soul the experience of raw trust without answers. It awakens the ache for a mediator. And it models the relentless insistence that, even in the silence, God must be good.

So, none of this is philosophical argument, but rather, it is relational speech.

The poetic structure is not trying to resolve a debate; it is trying to evoke the raw emotions that accompany covenant intimacy when confronted with God's sovereignty. Poetry becomes the language of what it feels like to love God when everything collapses. In that sense, Job's inner world is not being destroyed by suffering, it is being shaped by it. And the reader is being shaped as well.

So, as the poetry unfolds, it trains the reader to recognize the cry of the righteous, the longing for justice, the desire for a mediator, the weakness of human insight, and the immensity of God's glory. And in this way, Job's laments themselves become a kind of spiritual revelation.

I would further argue that Job's poetic laments prove his intimacy with God. His lament is not a failure of faith, it is the expression of faith. Because only true intimacy produces the boldness to question God with the honesty that speaks without fear, the anguish that still reaches toward Him, the longing for a Mediator, and the confidence in God's character despite the silence. These are not marks of a man losing his faith; they are the marks of a man who knows God deeply.

And that is the difference between Job and his friends. The friends speak *at* God as Job speaks *to* God. That alone tells us which one truly understands Him.

Job as the Psychological Center of Wisdom Literature

When we place Job alongside Proverbs and Ecclesiastes, a remarkable pattern emerges. Job sits alongside them as the crisis point of biblical wisdom; the moment where the tidy order of Proverbs and the weary honesty of Ecclesiastes collide inside a single human life.

Proverbs speaks with confidence that says, "Live wisely and it will go well."

It presents wisdom in its ideal form, where righteousness leads to blessing and wickedness leads to ruin. Its worldview is clean, ordered, and consistent.

Ecclesiastes, however, seems to speak with a sense of disillusionment that says, "Life doesn't always work like that."

It exposes the cracks in human understanding, and it reminds us that the world is vapor—hevel—and that even the wise cannot force life into predictable patterns. Its worldview is honest about the limits of human observation and the frustration of unmet expectations.

And then comes Job, who says, "Now watch a righteous man stand in the crucible between them."

We can think of it this way: Proverbs tells us to *"Live wisely and all will go well."* While Ecclesiastes says, "Life will break your expectations and expose the limits of human wisdom." But Job positions both to put an actual human soul in the middle of these two realities and see what happens internally.

This is why Job is not merely wisdom literature, but rather, it is wisdom literature functioning as psychological formation. It does not simply teach wisdom; it shapes wisdom within the reader.

Job's internal battle becomes the laboratory for this formation. So, Job is not just a man suffering; he is the entire human condition placed under a microscope. His struggle is every person's struggle who has ever tried to reconcile what they know about God with what they experience in the world, and what they feel within themselves.

This is why Job stands at the psychological center of biblical wisdom. It shows us that wisdom is not merely memorizing Proverbs, just as wisdom is not only despairing with Ecclesiastes. Wisdom is what remains when everything collapses and the soul still says, "I want God, even in the dark."

And it is also why Job both structurally and thematically stands near the Bible's center. Because it is the beating heart of the soul's journey toward God.

Job is wisdom in its testing. And it asks the question no other wisdom book dares to confront head-on of what happens when someone truly righteous endures the chaos Ecclesiastes laments, and must decide whether to hold onto the God Proverbs proclaims?

Job, therefore, becomes the human psyche wrestling between:

- what he knows about God (Proverbs)
- what he experiences in reality (Ecclesiastes)
- what he feels in his soul (the poetry and dialogues)
- what is true in heaven (the prologue)
- what is resolved by God (the whirlwind)

This is why Job is not only a theological masterpiece; it is also a psychological one. It does not simply teach us about wisdom, it forms the mind, confronts the emotions, and reshapes the heart. It reveals that true wisdom is born not in certainty or despair, but in the space where both collapse and the soul still reaches for God.

Job shows us what the journey of the righteous truly looks like when the world breaks, the heavens fall silent, and yet the longing for God refuses to die. It is wisdom that refuses to let go of God, even when the world gives us every reason to do so.

Elihu as the Literary and Theological Turning Point

Finally, Elihu remains one of the most misunderstood figures in the entire book of Job. He appears suddenly, speaks at length, and then disappears the moment God speaks, yet the narrative treats him with a level of nuance that demands our attention. His role is not incidental, nor is he simply another voice in the debate. Within the structure of the book, Elihu functions as both a literary device and a symbolic presence. He stands at the very hinge of the narrative, becoming the literal and philosophical transition point between the collapse of human wisdom and the unveiling of divine revelation.

Unlike the three friends, Elihu is never condemned by God. In fact, scripture goes out of its way to single out the trio of friends as those who "have not spoken rightly," (Job 42:7) but Elihu's name is conspicuously absent from the rebuke. He is not grouped with the false comforters, nor is he treated as an adversarial voice. Instead, he occupies a distinct category of his own, and one set apart from the failed explanations that preceded him. His speech prepares the reader for what comes next, serving as a kind of bridge into the whirlwind itself.

Elihu represents something emerging, and something transitional. As the younger man among them, he embodies the new generation; the voice that rises when the elders have exhausted their wisdom and found themselves unable to defend God rightly. But his youth is not a flaw; it is part of the symbolic framework. He also represents the fresh conscience awakened in the midst of suffering, the hunger for true intimacy with God, and the moment when human limitation gives way to a deeper longing for revelation.

Within his speeches, Elihu begins to articulate a kind of truth that the friends never approached. He does not accuse Job of hidden sin, nor does he reduce God to a formulaic dispenser of reward and punishment. Instead, Elihu argues that God is righteous, that God communicates through suffering, and that God's voice is often unnoticed because people are not listening for it. His theology is not perfect, but it is pointed in the right direction. He speaks of a God who is more active, more present, and more relational than the mechanical deity of the friends.

And then God arrives.

The entrance of the whirlwind does not correct Elihu the way it corrects the friends. Instead, God's appearance affirms that Elihu and Job were arguing toward the real God, the One who transcends human systems and refuses to be contained by simplistic doctrine. The friends spoke of a predictable deity made in their own image; Elihu, however, pointed toward a God whose sovereignty, mystery, and nearness cannot be reduced to equations.

Elihu's role, therefore, is not merely meant to fill a space between the dialogues and God's speech. He is the threshold. The moment where the narrative shifts from human attempts at explanation to divine self-revelation. He is the rising voice that signals God is near, and the final note before the whirlwind tears open the horizon.

Elihu stands where human wisdom ends and spiritual wisdom begins. His presence prepares both Job and the reader to recognize the God who is about to speak; not the god of formulas, but the God who enters storms, upends assumptions, and reveals Himself on His own terms.

Reading The Book as It Invites Us To

When we step back and consider the literary structure of Job in its fullness, with its prose and its poetry, its heavenly vantage point and its earthly struggle, we begin to understand why this book resists every attempt to flatten it. Job refuses to be reduced to a simple explanation of suffering or a moral tale with clean resolutions. Its very form is its own message. Its architecture is its theology. And the book itself is a living tension designed to shape the reader, not merely inform them.

Job is a narrative that opens in heaven, descends into the chaos of human experience, and then rises again when God speaks from the whirlwind. It pulls us into that descent intentionally, teaching us how to wrestle, how to listen, and how to hold both the ache of earth and the clarity of heaven at the same time. By moving us between prose and poetry, the author trains our spiritual instincts. We learn how to sit with mystery, how to recognize the voice of the righteous sufferer, how to discern the difference between formula and faith, and how to wait for the God who speaks in His own time.

And this is why the structure matters so deeply. Job forms the kind of reader who can encounter God without demanding control. It teaches us to linger in the silence rather than flee from it, to question without abandoning trust, and to feel deeply without losing sight of spiritual reality. It is, therefore, no accident that the book ends where it began, in prose. For after walking through the storm, the reader returns to the clarity of heaven's perspective. But now, the return feels different. Now, we carry the weight of all we have felt with Job, and the wisdom that has been forged through the tension.

This is why it is essential for the reader to understand the structure by which this story is written. For If we do not understand the book's structure, we can easily misunderstand everything that happens inside it. But once we see how the narrative is built, we are able to enter the story on its own terms, ready to sit with Job, to confront the adversary's question, and to listen for the God who answers from the whirlwind.

Job, then, invites us into a kind of wisdom that cannot be memorized, or domesticated. It is wisdom learned in the dark, shaped by longing, refined through honesty, and anchored in the character of God.

NOTES

NOTES

CHAPTER THREE

*Broken Wisdom, Inner Psychology, and the Limits of
Secondhand Faith*

When most people read the book of Job, they imagine the friends as
little more than narrative obstacles, or flat characters who enter the story
to say all the wrong things. Sermons tend to package them neatly as the
bad guys, or religious legalists, heartless advisors, or simply as the example
of what not to say to someone who is suffering. And while it is true that
their speeches are ultimately rebuked by God, that is not the full picture.
The friends are far more complex, and the role they play in Job's spiritual
formation, and by extension, in the reader's formation, is far more revealing than the caricatures suggest.

Job's friends represent the limits of religion, the limits of tradition,
and the limits of secondhand knowledge of God. They embody the kind
of wisdom that works well enough in theory but collapses under the
weight of real suffering. And this collapse is intentional. The author of
Job is exposing not just their flawed counsel, but the fault lines in every
human attempt to explain God without actually knowing Him.

The truth is far more nuanced, in my opinion, than the typical "friends bad, Job good" reading. While the friends do indeed get things wrong, they are not wrong in everything. And the way they are wrong is deeply instructive. Some of what they say is true, but misapplied.

They speak genuine proverbs, genuine observations about the moral universe, and genuine truths about God's justice. But they wield these truths like blunt instruments, and tools of analysis rather than tools of compassion.

At the same time, some of what they say is false, even though it sounds pious. Their theology often "sounds right," because it borrows the vocabulary of righteousness, justice, and God's order. But their conclusions are rooted in fear, not revelation, and in formula apart from relationship.

So, their theology is often technically orthodox, but their hearts are blind. They say the kinds of things religious people have always said through statements that work in calm settings and controlled environments, but they cannot see beyond their own frameworks. They do not see Job. Nor do they do not see the heart of God. They only see their system.

And because of this, their conclusions collapse against Job's circumstances. However, that collapse is the point. Job is the test case that exposes the fragility of secondhand faith, assumptions about how God should act, and rigid doctrines that have never been tested in the fire.

This is why Job's friends are so important to the structure of the book. They function not merely as external characters, but as mirrors reflecting the fractured ways humanity tries to make sense of God. Their speeches reveal the inner psychology of the soul under pressure.

Because the truth is, Job is not only debating them literally; he is also debating them internally. Each friend represents a kind of wisdom tradition, but also a kind of internal voice—a fractured soul-component—that rises up when suffering disrupts our categories.

The friends, therefore, show us what happens when wisdom lacks intimacy. When theology lacks encounter. When we try to defend God instead of knowing Him. When our frameworks are trusted more than God's character. And when our ideas remain untouched by the mystery of suffering.

So, as we approach their speeches, we must resist the instinct to dismiss them as shallow thinkers. They are not shallow. They are sincere, articulate, and deeply rooted in the wisdom traditions of their time. And that is precisely why they are dangerous. They represent what faith looks like when it is inherited but untested, confident but unexamined, and orthodox but untransformed.

In this chapter, we will explore their voices on two levels:

- as representatives of broken wisdom traditions,
- and as reflections of the fractured, internal dialogue of the human soul.

Religion and Tradition

It's important to note that Job's friends do not emerge from a vacuum. They are the products of a religious system; one shaped by inherited theology, rigid structures, and moral formulas passed down through generations. In many ways, they embody the best expressions of the wisdom tradition available at the time. They speak confidently, eloquently, and with the full weight of cultural expectation behind them.

And yet, for all their certainty, they crumble in the presence of a suffering man whose experience does not fit their categories.

The wisdom they offer is not born from encounter. It is born from inheritance. They have inherited their theology as truths passed down like family heirlooms that have been polished by repetition but never tested in the fire.

Their worldview thus rests on rigid structure, and an orderly system where everything fits neatly, provided nothing unexpected ever happens. So their counsel relies on simple cause-and-effect equations by which the righteous prosper, the wicked perish, everything else is an anomaly to be explained away.

And beneath it all lies a simplified religious equation through a kind of spiritual mathematics they believe governs the universe. This is the religion of assumption and the theology of tradition.

This is the wisdom of those who know what they have been told, but have never wrestled with God themselves. And this is precisely why God rebukes them in the end.

Their confidence is solid, but superficial. And they can recite truths about God, but they cannot recognize the God standing behind those truths.

This distinction is not lost on those who have studied the book across the centuries. Early Jewish commentators saw the friends as representatives of a broken or incomplete wisdom tradition; where they were true in pieces, but distorted in practice. The Church Fathers often interpreted them as the voices of cold religion, the kind that prized being right more than being righteous. Modern scholars consistently identify them as carriers of retribution theology, and defenders of a rigid worldview that demands the universe operate according to predictable moral mechanics.

Their reliance on formula, tradition, and cause-and-effect religion is precisely what makes them incapable of comprehending Job's suffering. They assume righteousness guarantees blessing because that is what their system taught them. Notice how they do not adjust their theology, they simply adjust their accusation.

Their wisdom, then, becomes rigid, doctrinally tidy, and ultimately spiritually dead. In other words, they know *about* God, but they do not *know* Him. That is the heart of their failure. Their theology contains truth, but it is truth detached from relationship. Their doctrine may be orthodox, but it is lifeless. And their categories are neat, but they cannot accommodate mystery.

It is the same critique Jesus leveled against the Pharisees when He called them whitewashed tombs, an indictment so severe it only intensified their hatred toward Him. (Matt 23:27-28)

Psychologically, this distinction is crucial. Job's friends reveal the chasm between secondhand faith and relational faith. Secondhand faith knows the rules; relational faith knows the One who wrote them. The former can argue theology, but only the latter can survive the storm. And that difference is what drives the conflict between Job and his three friends throughout the majority of the book.

Archetypes of Arguments Within the Soul

As mentioned earlier, their speeches are not only external dialogues with Job; they are mirrors reflecting the fractured inner world of a righteous man trying to make sense of his own suffering. Each friend represents something far deeper than a historical personality. They embody a kind of archetypal soul-voice through patterns of human reasoning, instinctive coping mechanisms, and spiritual distortions that rise to the surface when suffering threatens to unravel everything we thought we knew about God.

So, while Job is debating outwardly with three men, he is also debating inwardly with three parts of himself. Their words expose the internal storm that rages inside any believer who has walked into the darkest points of their life. The friends become personified expressions of Job's own struggle, and voices that echo inside the mind when suffering refuses to yield answers.

They are not simply antagonists in the narrative; they are the familiar inner voices humans instinctively lean on when faith is stretched beyond its limits. They embody the broken strategies people use to regain control when life spirals into chaos.

Thus, at a higher level, the friends correspond to different symbolic archetypes:

- Eliphaz – the mystical tradition, the intuition-based religion that relies on inner impressions, spiritual experiences, or "what I feel God must be like."

- Bildad – the traditionalist, the voice of inherited beliefs, cultural memory, and established doctrines that refuse to bend even when reality demands it.

- Zophar – the moral absolutist, the harsh internal critic that assumes suffering must be deserved, a voice soaked in self-condemnation and rigid moral equations.

Together, these three form a triad of fractured human reasoning, and three ways the soul grasps for stability when confronted with the unexplainable.

And then there is Elihu, a different kind of voice entirely, as we discussed in the previous chapter. He represents youthful idealism, the emerging awakened self, and the part of the inner man that begins to break free from the old systems without yet fully understanding the new. He is not yet wisdom, but he is closer to revelation than the others. His presence signals that something in Job that is shifting, and preparing him for the encounter with God.

Through their voices, Job is forced to confront the theological, emotional, and psychological frameworks that no longer hold under the pressure of pain.

Therefore, their speeches are not merely arguments, they are the anatomy of the human condition under trial.

Eliphaz — The Voice of Spiritualized Reason

When the dialogues begin, Eliphaz speaks first. He is likely the oldest of the three, and his position as the opening voice establishes the tone for the friends' entire theological framework. Eliphaz carries himself as the "mystic" of the group; someone who appeals to spiritual experiences, visions in the night, intuitive impressions, and moral logic. His speeches blend spiritual language with a kind of confident moral certainty. Outwardly, he appears wise. While inwardly, he is the embodiment of spiritualized reason, and the instinct to interpret suffering through a predetermined religious grid.

But beneath the surface, Eliphaz represents something far more intimate and familiar. He is the psychological voice within the human soul that insists, "Pain must always have a reason." He personifies the moralistic conscience, and the inner religious voice that tells us God runs the world on a strict reward-and-punishment system. In Eliphaz's worldview, suffering is not a mystery; it is a moral equation. If Job is suffering, then Job must be at fault. Not because Eliphaz delights in accusing him, but because the idea of undeserved suffering feels too frightening for him to accept.

Thus Eliphaz reveals the soul's fearful desire for control that says, "If suffering is predictable, life is safer."

So, if righteousness guarantees blessing, and wrongdoing guarantees pain, then the universe feels manageable, almost domesticated. But the moment suffering enters without an identifiable cause, the internal world begins to panic. Eliphaz gives voice to that panic.

His inner script is the same script many believers whisper to themselves in moments of crisis:

- "I must have done something wrong."
- "Maybe God is punishing me."
- "Bad things don't just happen."

These are not merely theological errors; they are psychological reflexes. They arise when the human soul grasps for stability in a world suddenly stripped of answers. Eliphaz's speeches sound authoritative because he speaks from this deep, instinctive place in which the conscience is desperate to impose order on chaos.

Yet spiritually, this becomes a distortion.

Eliphaz takes spiritual logic and bends it into self-condemnation. He turns moral intuition into accusation. And he represents the part of the soul that tries to explain the unexplainable and reduce the vast mystery of God into a set of manageable formulas. It is an intuition-based religion that talks often about God but still lacks intimacy with Him. In other words, Eliphaz can describe visions and recount spiritual impressions, but he does not know God the way Job does. He knows only the system.

This is precisely why Job argues with him so fiercely. Job's relationship with God contradicts Eliphaz's tidy framework. Job knows, from lived intimacy, that God is not confined to a rigid cause-and-effect world. He knows that righteousness does not guarantee immunity from suffering. He also knows that God's goodness does not collapse simply because circumstances do. And so, when Job debates Eliphaz, he is not merely correcting a friend, he is confronting the inner religious voice that rises within every believer in seasons of darkness.

Eliphaz whispers the same question the adversary whispered in the heavenly council, but in a subtler tone that says, "Maybe God's goodness toward you was just an illusion."

And this is why Job refuses to accept Eliphaz's arguments. Because to agree with him would require Job to betray what he knows to be true about God. It would require him to exchange relational knowledge for spiritualized formulas. Thus, Job's resistance is the resistance of a tested faith pushing back against the simplistic logic of fear.

Eliphaz is not the villain of the story; he is the voice of the religious conscience under strain. But Job's journey requires that voice to be confronted—and ultimately silenced—before he is prepared to hear the only voice that can truly interpret his suffering: the voice of God Himself.

Bildad — The Voice of Traditional Fear

If Eliphaz speaks with the calm authority of mystical logic, Bildad arrives with a very different tone. He appeals almost exclusively to the weight of tradition, the wisdom of ancestors, and the fear of consequences. His speeches are filled with references to "the ancients," as though history itself is the ultimate proof of his argument. For Bildad, tradition is not simply a guide, it is the boundary line of safety. Anything outside it feels dangerous and even threatening.

In the psychological dimension, Bildad is the voice within the soul that insists:

- "This is how it has always been."
- "These are the rules."
- "If you step outside the lines, you suffer."

He closely represents the anxious inner child: the part of us that clings to old structures because they feel familiar, predictable, and secure. So, while Eliphaz uses spiritual logic to steady himself, Bildad reaches for the comfort of inherited patterns. His worldview depends on the belief that the past has already charted every possible outcome, and thus deviation can only lead to disaster.

Bildad embodies a kind of legalism wrapped in tradition. His arguments are not rooted in revelation but in collective memory. He appeals to group consensus because he fears being wrong alone. His theology is less about truth and more about stability. In other words, it is less about God's character and more about protecting himself from the terror of uncertainty.

At the emotional level, Bildad is more immature than Eliphaz. His fear is closer to the surface, and because of this, he often speaks more harshly, more loudly, and with more urgency. When someone feels internally unstable, they compensate externally with volume. Bildad shouts because he is afraid. His certainty is a mask for anxiety.

He is also the voice that tells a suffering soul, "If bad things happen, it must be because you failed."

Not out of malice, but out of fear. Because if suffering can happen unjustly, then the world is not safe. And Bildad cannot bear a world that is not safe.

Spiritually, Bildad's distortion is subtle but devastating. He instinctively shrinks God down to the size of human systems so that He makes God predictable, controllable, and institutional.

In Bildad's theology, God's justice is indistinguishable from the mechanical workings of tradition. God becomes the enforcer of inherited structures rather than the sovereign, relational, living God who cannot be boxed into human patterns. Bildad's God is a projection of human fear, not the God who speaks out of the whirlwind.

This is why Job argues with him. Job recognizes the deep fear at the core of Bildad's thinking, and he refuses to allow that fear to shape his own understanding of God. Job has known the Lord too intimately to collapse His character into tradition, moral formulas, or the anxieties of the community.

So when Job debates Bildad, he is not merely dismantling a friend's argument. He is confronting his own temptation to retreat into fear-based religion. He is resisting the internal instinct to hide inside clichés rather than wrestle honestly with God. Thus, Bildad is the part of the soul that longs to run back to the familiar when faith becomes painful. Thus, Job's refusal to follow him is an act of courage.

Bildad teaches us that fear masquerading as wisdom is one of the greatest dangers in suffering. But Job teaches us that true faith never hides behind borrowed answers. It presses forward, even when it is trembling, to seek the God who cannot be contained by the past.

Zophar — The Voice of Self-Righteous Certainty

So, if Eliphaz speaks with mystical confidence and Bildad with anxious traditionalism, Zophar enters the dialogue like a hammer. He is the harshest of the three: accusatory, dogmatic, and forceful. He does not appeal to visions or ancestral wisdom. He appeals to certainty. Zophar "knows" what God should say. He "knows" how the universe should function. And in his mind, Job's suffering can only mean one thing: guilt. Deep, hidden, and unconfessed guilt.

Psychologically, Zophar is the inner critic, the self-condemning voice that emerges when pain has stripped away clarity and all that remains is the echo of shame. His words mirror the internal accusations many believers whisper to themselves in moments of despair:

"You're worse than you think."

"If only God would speak, He would condemn you."

"You need to repent for things you didn't even do."

Zophar represents the perfectionist self, and the part of the soul that assumes God is perpetually angry, disappointed, and always ready to strike. He embodies the punitive superego, the internal judge that demands self-punishment even when no sin exists. His voice is the voice of shame, and the instinct to blame oneself when suffering defies explanation.

This is why Zophar is so aggressive. He is not merely attacking Job; he is articulating the darkest, most accusatory part of Job's own internal world. Zophar externalizes the voice that says, "If something went wrong, it must be your fault." But his certainty is not born from truth, it is born from fear masquerading as morality. When the world shatters, the inner critic would rather accept false guilt than face the terror of un-answered suffering.

Spiritually, Zophar falls into a fatal distortion that equates God with an inflexible and punitive judge. He projects his own inner condemnation onto God and mistakes the voice of shame for the voice of the Almighty. This is why Zophar's speeches feel so suffocating. He speaks as if he is defending God, but he is only defending his own wounded theology.

Job recognizes this distortion immediately. Even in his anguish, he knows—deep in his soul—that God is more merciful than Zophar claims. He knows God's character is better, richer, and more compassionate than what Zophar's cold theology can comprehend. Job may not understand his suffering, but he understands God's nature. And that is enough to refute Zophar's accusations.

Thus, Job's arguments against Zophar are not merely arguments against a friend. They are arguments against the voice inside himself that wants to collapse into shame. Job is defending God's true nature against the dark distortions of his own wounded heart. He is fighting not only a theological battle but a psychological one against self-condemnation, despair, and against the internal critic that insists God must be angry because the world has fallen apart.

Zophar shows us the most dangerous lie suffering can tell that, "God is condemning you."

But Job's resistance shows us the courage of faith that says "No. God is better than that."

Elihu — The Emerging True Self

Elihu then enters the book suddenly, almost out of nowhere. He is not one of the three friends, nor does he share their theological rigidity. He is a fourth voice—a surprising, disruptive presence—and his arrival marks a decisive turning point in the entire narrative. The structure of Job slows, shifts, and lifts in tone the moment he speaks. His voice signals that something inside Job has begun to awaken.

Elihu represents the younger voice of spiritual awakening, and the part of the soul that is finally ready for revelation. After long cycles of arguments that led nowhere and explanations that only deepened the ache, Elihu rises like the cry of spiritual longing within a weary heart. He embodies the desire to know God for oneself, without filters, formulas, or inherited expectations. He is hungry for authenticity over tradition.

And it is this hunger that sets Elihu apart from the others.

Elihu is passionate for God. His words burn with urgency and conviction. He is dissatisfied with shallow answers, both the harsh condemnations of the friends and the despairing confusion of Job. He refuses to accept either extreme. And he critiques both sides not out of arrogance, but out of zeal for righteousness and a deep conviction that God is bigger than all their arguments.

When Elihu speaks, we hear a soul longing for truth, for clarity, and for a God who is more than what man can understand. His speech is bold, emotional, and unfiltered. There is frustration in him, but also hope. And there is honesty in him, just as there is reverence. But most importantly, Elihu begins introducing themes that God Himself will later affirm in the whirlwind through God's transcendence, His nearness, and unbounded sovereignty.

Psychologically, Elihu represents the moment the soul shifts from intellectual argument to desperate spiritual hunger. This is the deeper breakthrough. Job has spent chapters defending himself, countering accusations, and wrestling with the assumptions imposed upon him. But

Elihu embodies the interior movement from debate to longing, and from wanting answers to wanting God.

Elihu is the moment the soul says, "I want to know God for real."

He is the proto-disciple, the one who rises up between old structures and new revelation. He is the modern believer wrestling with inherited theology, caught between tradition and experience, aching for a God who seems silent yet undeniably present. Elihu is the part of Job that questions God's silence but refuses to fall into despair. He is the internal voice that rejects superficial answers and reaches toward intimacy.

Elihu also symbolizes something broader through the emergence of a new generation seeking God for themselves. Not content with second-hand faith, with ancestral formulas, nor with the safety of rigid tradition. Elihu is the cry of a generation saying, "I must see God with my own eyes."

And God answers that hunger. Not because Elihu's theology is flawless, but because he expresses himself perfectly. And because his cry is aimed at the real God, not at preserving a system, defending a tradition, or propping up a worldview.

Elihu is the dawn breaking before the whirlwind. He is the internal awakening that prepares the heart for encounter, and the spark of revelation that signals God is near.

What This Means for Job's Inner Life

Through the speeches, we watch a man confronting every instinct the human soul reaches for in suffering: the instinct to blame himself, to retreat into tradition, to collapse into shame, and finally, to reach toward God with an honest cry. Job's dialogues reveal a man who is fighting not to lose who he knows God to be. He is speaking from relationship, even when that relationship feels unbearably strained. He refuses to surrender his knowledge of God's character, though every voice around him (and within him) urges him to reinterpret reality through fear, guilt, or tradition.

Job's struggle is the struggle of covenant faith itself. And it is covenant faith that is relational. It clings to God even when explanations fail. It laments, cries, questions, and it wrestles. But most importantly, it begs for God's presence. These are not signs of unbelief; they are the expressions of intimacy under pressure. Anyone can talk about God when life is stable. But only the one who knows God cries out to Him when the world collapses. So, lament is not rebellion; it is fidelity in the dark.

By contrast, the friends' faith is rigid. Their worldview is built on a simple equation that if you do well, you receive blessing. And if you are suffering, then it is because of sin.

This is not covenant faith. This is legalism. It is the attempt to control God through moral predictability, to reduce relationship to a system, and to make suffering manageable by making it deserved. Legalism cannot survive mystery because it breaks the moment life breaks the pattern.

But Job's faith survives *because* it is relational. It is built on *who* God is, not on *what* Job receives. And as Job wrestles with these inner voices, he reveals what true righteousness looks like: not the absence of questions, but the refusal to let any inner distortion redefine God's character.

Job's inner life becomes the battleground where covenant faith proves itself stronger than inherited formulas. And in that battleground, God is preparing him for the one thing the friends could never imagine and the inner critic could never predict.

CHAPTER THREE

The Human Condition Without a Mediator

At a deeper level, Job's arguments are not merely directed toward three companions sitting in the ashes beside him. He is arguing with the entire human condition's attempts to understand God without a Mediator. His struggle exposes the collapse of every human approach to theology that depends on intellect, tradition, or moral formulas alone. Without a Mediator, the human mind reaches its limits very quickly, and the friends represent every one of those limits.

Job's dialogues sound less like a debate between four men and more like the thundering echo of the soul trying to interpret God through its own fractured faculties. When we listen closely, we hear guilt, doubt, anger, tradition, faith, longing, fear, righteousness, and memory of God's goodness all colliding inside him. They are the very real movements of a heart straining to hold onto God in the dark.

This is why the arguments of the friends fail so spectacularly. Their "wisdom" represents the failure of human reasoning apart from intimacy. When the soul tries to build theology without encounter, it inevitably creates a god made in its own image. Job's friends illustrate this perfectly. Their explanations are intellectually tidy but spiritually barren.

And this is precisely why Job's faith stands out as something different. Even in confusion, and even in anguish, he refuses to reduce God to the size of their arguments. As he wrestles with the shadows of theology, he begins to sense—not fully, but prophetically—that he needs someone beyond himself. His longing breaks through the constraints of his friends' systems and reaches toward a Mediator. Long before the Incarnation, Job's heart was crying out for Christ.

He hints at this Mediator repeatedly:

"Even now my Witness is in heaven." (Job 16:19)

"I know my Redeemer lives." (Job 19:25)

"I need One to lay His hand on us both." (Job 9:33)

These are the cries of a soul realizing the inadequacy of human wisdom and the necessity of divine intervention. Job is not just wrestling with types of theology, but he is longing for the God behind them. He is longing for someone who can stand between heaven and earth, someone who can interpret God's heart and bear the weight of human suffering.

In this sense, Job's struggle becomes a prophetic anticipation of Christ. His longing exposes the void that only the Mediator can fill. He shows us what the human condition looks like when left to its own resources, and why those resources inevitably fail. Job's need becomes our need. His cry becomes the cry of every heart that tries to know God through intellect alone. Thus, Job reveals that without a Mediator, theology becomes accusation, tradition becomes bondage, mysticism becomes confusion, and logic becomes condemnation.

But with a Mediator everything changes.

Job does not know His name yet. But he knows the ache that Christ alone can satisfy.

When God Finally Speaks

Throughout the dialogues, Job appears to be arguing with three companions, but by now the reader understands the deeper truth that Job is wrestling with the very architecture of his own soul. Every speech is a collision of fractured internal voices, all struggling to interpret God in the silence. Job's suffering has fractured him, and his speeches are the sound of those fractures clashing against one another.

And then God speaks.

The whirlwind is not simply the arrival of God's authority; it is the moment of integration. The presence of God does what no argument and no logic could do. When God finally speaks, the fragmented parts of Job's inner life are gathered, confronted, and healed under the weight of revelation.

In the whirlwind, Job's internal voices are brought under the revelation of God's glory. And the inner fragmentation ends, not because Job receives explanations, but because he encounters the One who transcends every explanation.

The transformation of Job does not come from tidy theological answers or intellectual clarity. It comes from presence, revelation, and encounter. Job changes because the voice of the living God steps into the chaos of his inner world and reorders it from the inside out. Every voice that once demanded answers is silenced by the voice that *is* the answer.

So, as God speaks, the friends' frameworks are exposed as far too small, too mechanical, and too brittle to contain the vastness of God's being. Their systems shatter in the presence of the God who cannot be boxed into tradition or logic. Everything they relied on is revealed as insufficient. But Job's intimacy—his stubborn refusal to let go of God, even in the dark—is vindicated.

He was right to wrestle. He was right to cry out. He was right to reject the formulas. And he was right to hold onto the God he knew, even when he could not feel Him.

So, when God speaks, Job's soul, though broken, exhausted, pulled in four different directions, finally comes to rest. The war within him ends. Not because his circumstances have been restored yet, but because his vision has. The God he longed for now stands before him. And that is enough.

Job's transformation therefore reveals the heart of the book in which suffering does not destroy the righteous, it reveals the depths of their relationship with God. The whirlwind does not answer Job's questions; it answers Job. And the soul that refused to let go of God finally finds rest in the God who never let go of him.

The Soul in the Ashes

By the end of the dialogues, it is my hope that the reader no longer sees Job's friends as mere supporting characters. They represent everything the human heart reaches for when the world collapses. And that Job's conversations with them show us that the deepest battles of faith are fought inside the human soul long before they are expressed in words.

His arguments with each companion expose internal fissures and unaddressed assumptions that suffering has forced to the surface. In this sense, the ash heap is not only a geographical location, it is the symbolic landscape of Job's inner life.

Yet through all this internal turbulence, one truth rises again and again that Job refuses to abandon relationship. Even when every inner voice tells him to surrender, Job refuses. His faith is not clean, composed, or theologically tidy. It is raw and fierce. But it is the desperate cry of a heart that knows God too deeply to accept a false picture of Him.

This is why Job stands apart.

Job is not being tested on his ability to produce correct theology; he is being refined through the crucible of intimacy. His longing for God grows louder than every other voice. His ache becomes the very place where revelation will land. And the book prepares us to see that the answer to suffering is not found in human wisdom at all, it is found in encounter.

In the next chapter, we step into Job's lament, and we begin to understand why only God's presence can heal what suffering fractures.

NOTES

NOTES

CHAPTER FOUR

Job's Lament

There is a common misconception, in my opinion, that to wrestle with God—to express anger, frustration, uncertainty, or brokenness—is somehow conflated with irreverence. That as believers, we must present ourselves a certain way when we approach the throne of grace, or risk undermining God's holiness. Many have absorbed the idea that coming before God requires a curated posture in which we must be emotionally controlled, theologically correct, or spiritually "polished". Anything less can feel risky, irreverent, or spiritually suspect.

And though lamentation is often acknowledged as an honest expression of the human condition, it is frequently treated as something that must eventually be corrected. But the truth is, God's holiness is not threatened by human honesty. Rather, He honors it. And I would argue that the refusal to wrestle often reveals distance, not reverence.

Lament, is not the opposite of faith. It is faith in its most vulnerable posture. It takes faith to cry out to a God you cannot see. It takes faith to bring anguish into His presence rather than burying it in silence. And it takes faith to believe you are still heard when heaven feels unresponsive and the darkness stretches on without explanation. Unbelief walks away when lament chooses to stay.

At its core, lament is the language of those who refuse to sever the relationship. It is faith that insists God hears even when the world offers no confirmation. Faith that trusts God sees even when suffering obscures every sign of His nearness. It believes that God will answer, even if the timing feels unbearable or incomprehensible. And it is faith that dares to bring the darkest, most unfiltered cries of the human heart before Him without editing or disguising it.

This is why Job's lament is not rebellion. It is intimacy stripped of all pretense. Job is not cursing God; he is clinging to Him with what little strength remains, even as his understanding collapses. So, his anguish signals the desperate insistence that God must still be there and that the relationship must still matter, even if nothing makes sense anymore.

But this is precisely what unsettles so many readers. Job says things we would never dare say aloud. He voices confusion, despair, longing, and protest without softening the edges. He speaks words that feel theologically uncomfortable, even dangerous. Yet God never rebukes him for speaking this way. Instead, God calls him blameless. Not because Job's words were neat or doctrinally refined, but because they were honest.

Job tells the truth of his soul to the God he loves. And in Scripture, truth spoken before God is never treated as irreverence; it is treated as worship. Thus, his lament becomes his offering, and the sacrifice of a heart that refuses to pretend, refuses to sanitize its pain, and refuses to replace honesty with hollow piety. It is the soul approaching God with nothing but truth, even when that truth is cracked, trembling, and soaked in tears.

Through this, Job teaches us something both uncomfortable and liberating in that God is not offended by human weakness; He is drawn to it. He is not threatened by grief; He enters into it. And He does not silence the anguished cry, but eagerly meets the one who dares to cry at all. The book of Job confronts us with this reality again and again because faith is not proven by composure, but by persistence.

In truth, Job's lament is intimate because it is unfiltered. He brings the full weight of his inner world into God's presence because he believes God alone can bear it. That is what makes him righteous because it's not the calmness of his theology, but the courage of his honesty.

But Job is not alone in this way of speaking. Scripture is filled with faithful voices who cry out to God in language that, on the surface, sounds contradictory, unsettling, or even accusatory. Yet these voices are not rebuked. They are preserved and even canonized, which should tell us something important about how God hears the cries of those who love Him.

David, a man after God's own heart, accuses God of sleeping. He pleads as though God has turned away, as though He has forgotten His covenant, as though the silence must mean absence (Psalm 44:23-24). David does not sanitize his prayers or softens his anguish. He brings his felt reality straight into God's presence and speaks it without apology. And God does not distance Himself from David for this. He draws nearer.

Jeremiah goes even further. In the depths of his prophetic anguish, he dares to describe God as "a deceptive stream," as a warrior who fails to come through when needed most (Jeremiah 15:18). But these are not the words of a man who has abandoned God. They are the words of a man who has been faithful enough to feel the weight of disappointment when obedience leads to pain rather than relief. Jeremiah's lament is not unbelief; it is the agony of intimacy strained by suffering.

Habakkuk, too, confronts God directly. He questions God's tolerance of injustice. He challenges the apparent delay of divine intervention. He dares to ask why God seems to stand idle while evil advances. And instead of rebuking him, God answers. Not because Habakkuk spoke politely, but because he spoke honestly. (Habakkuk 1:2-5)

And then there is Jesus.

On the cross, the Son of God Himself cries out, "My God, My God, why have You forsaken Me?" This is not a breakdown in faith. It is the culmination of covenantal trust carried into the deepest darkness imaginable. Jesus prays the words of Psalm 22 not to signal abandonment, but to give voice to suffering within relationship. The most intimate relationship in existence expresses itself through lament. But this is not irreverence, it is perfect intimacy expressing itself through perfect lament.

And biblical lament almost always sounds "wrong" to ears trained to value composure over communion. It unsettles those who confuse reverence with restraint and faith with emotional control. But lament only sounds wrong if we ignore the heart behind it. And the heart behind biblical lament is always the same. It is honest, unfiltered, courageous, and deeply relational.

These voices do not speak from distance. They speak from proximity. And they do not accuse God from outside the covenant; they cry out from within it. Thus lament, in Scripture, is never the language of those who have left God, it is the language of those who refuse to leave Him, even when everything in them aches.

Job stands in this sacred tradition, and his words are relationally spoken under unbearable strain. And Scripture does not silence these voices. It preserves them. Because God would rather receive an honest cry than a polished lie.

The Paradox of Lament

Lament gives voice to sorrow, confusion, and pain in ways that seem to contradict everything God has revealed about Himself. Job's words often sound like they stand in tension with God's character. And yet, that tension is the unavoidable collision between lived suffering and confessed belief.

Lament sounds contradictory because suffering itself is contradictory. It forces the soul to hold opposing realities at the same time. The heart says, I know God is good, while the body feels abandoned. The mind says, I trust Him, while the soul cannot make sense of what is happening. The spirit whispers, I believe, while the lips tremble with the cry, help my unbelief. These are not failures of faith. They are the fractures faith must endure in a broken world.

This is why lament cannot be reduced to systematic theology. It does not organize doctrine or resolve tension. It does not smooth out contradictions or answer questions cleanly. Lament is the human soul meeting God without pretense, without polish, and without the protection of tidy explanations. It is what happens when faith stops performing and starts speaking truth.

This is not an inferior form of prayer; it is the holiest form of prayer available to a suffering soul. It is prayer that refuses to lie in God's presence, and it is prayer that chooses relationship over reputation.

Thus, Lament becomes reverence expressed through paradox. It honors God not because it sounds beautiful, but because it tells the truth. It does not diminish God's holiness; it acknowledges His capacity to hold human pain without shattering the relationship.

This is precisely why God honors Job's lament and rejects the counsel of the friends. Job speaks from intimacy. His words rise out of lived relationship, covenant history, and a heart that knows God well enough to argue with Him. The friends, by contrast, speak from theory. They say many correct things about God, but they do so without relational knowledge. Their theology is accurate in fragments, but detached from encounter.

Job, on the other hand, says things that are theologically uncomfortable, even incorrect when measured in isolation. Yet they are spoken from deep covenant loyalty. His words are not calculated to protect an image of God; they are uttered because he trusts God enough to risk honesty. And that is why God later declares, "Job has spoken rightly of Me."

In the economy of God, honesty spoken in love outweighs correctness spoken without intimacy. Lament is reverence because it refuses to abandon God in the midst of contradiction. It stays, it speaks, and it trusts that God is strong enough to receive it.

What The Reader Is Invited Into

As we dive into the text, it becomes clear that Job is doing far more than presenting a theological problem to be solved for us as the reader. Yes, the text gives us structure. It gives us authorship questions, Hebrew poetry, and access to ancient wisdom traditions. It invites close reading, careful interpretation, and intellectual engagement. All of those matters. But the true invitation of the book is not academic; it is relational.

Job never steps out of dialogue with God. Even when his words are sharp, or when his questions burn, he keeps speaking to God. The friends, by contrast, slowly retreat into doctrine. They stop listening. They stop responding to Job as a person. And they stop addressing God directly as they begin speaking about Him instead. Their theology becomes a shield that protects them from the discomfort of relationship.

But Job stays in intimacy. He wrestles face-to-face while the friends hide behind their theology.

This is the line the book keeps drawing, again and again. Not between belief and unbelief, but between relationship and abstraction. Job's faith remains alive because it remains engaged. He does not protect God from his pain, nor does he protect himself from God. He brings his whole self into the relationship and refuses to disengage, even when everything in him is exhausted.

And this is the heart of the book's invitation to the reader.

Will you stay in dialogue when God feels silent? Will you remain in intimacy when your theology no longer explains your experience? Will you risk honesty over correctness?

The book of Job relentlessly suggests that God prefers anguished intimacy to polished certainty. He honors the embittered cry not because it is pleasant, but because it is relational. Thus, Job's lament is not rebellion; it is the fierce loyalty of a soul that will not walk away.

So, in the end, Job is not commended for having the right answers. He is commended for staying present. And the reader is invited to do the same.

Lament As Worship

Job is stripped of everything he knows literally and emotionally, and the world has crushed him under the weight of its injustice, yet Job's choice to cry out in lamentation is much more than an embittered cry as we've discussed. On a deeper level, Job's lament is worship. And his cries are hope that refuses to die, even when everything around him has collapsed.

This is covenantal intimacy.

In the story of Job, his worship is not found in songs or sacrifices, but in his relentless orientation toward God. Even when his words falter, his direction never changes.

And this is why God honors Job. His lament was worship because it placed God at the center of his pain rather than pushing Him to the margins.

Job teaches us that worship is not always beautiful. Sometimes it is fractured and raw. But when it rises from covenant loyalty and refuses to let go of God, it is holy.

God's Answer Through Presence

By the time we reach chapter 38, Job has long since exhausted the hope of tidy explanations. He has cried, argued, pleaded, and waited. But beneath all of that is a longing for the presence of God. And what God gives Job in the end is infinitely better than anything Job could have imagined asking for.

God gives Job Himself.

When God speaks from the whirlwind, He does not arrive with a lecture on the mechanics of suffering. He does not explain the heavenly courtroom, or justify His decisions. Nor does He not tell Job why any of this happened. Instead, He reveals who He is. And in doing so, He answers Job at the deepest level possible.

From the storm, God declares—without stating it directly—that He is the Master of both chaos and order. He governs the wild and the tame, the forces Job fears and the forces Job loves. He rules over the uncontrollable, the dangerous, the mysterious, and the beautiful. Nothing lies outside His care. Nothing escapes His attention. And nothing—least of all Job's suffering—exists beyond His sovereign presence.

God's speech is not meant to confuse Job; it is meant to reorient him. God is showing Job a world far larger than his pain, and a sovereignty far more intimate than Job ever imagined. He is saying, in effect, I am good in ways you cannot comprehend. I am involved in every detail, even when I am silent. And I have never left you. So, when God answers, He gives Job exactly what he has been asking for all along.

He shows up.

And that presence does everything that explanations never could. God's self-revelation heals Job where logic could not. It satisfies him where answers would have fallen short. It humbles him, not by shaming him, but by expanding his vision. It restores him from the inside out. It integrates the fractured parts of his soul that have been at war with one another. And it vindicates him, not because Job was right about everything, but because he was right to keep reaching for God.

God's self-revelation is the true resolution of the book. Not the restoration of wealth. Not the rebuke of the friends. Not even the answers Job never receives. The resolution is encounter and it is presence. The resolution is the living God stepping into the whirlwind of Job's pain and revealing Himself as sufficient.

And it is Job's lament that makes room for this encounter.

Job's honesty creates the relational space where God can reveal Himself most fully. His refusal to disengage and his willingness to bring truth rather than polish into God's presence is the doorway through which God enters.

So, the final message of Job's lament is not that suffering is explained, but that it is met. When the soul cries honestly, God answers honestly. And His answer is not information, but Himself.

His presence is the answer.

NOTES

NOTES

CHAPTER FIVE

The Real Question Behind the Book of Job

From the opening scenes of the book, the reader is decisively oriented toward a reality that feels somewhat unorthodox. The story begins by introducing a man in his present life, and then immediately draws the reader into the courtroom of heaven itself, revealing an alternate reality unfolding simultaneously. From there, the narrative places us inside an unusual heavenly dialogue.

Many assume that this "trial" exists because of the man named Job who is introduced at the beginning. But when the scene is examined carefully, it becomes clear that the trial unfolding in the book of Job is not primarily about Job's righteousness, hidden sin, or moral endurance. Job is not the defendant standing before a suspicious God. Rather, he is the ground on which a far greater accusation is being tested.

God Initiates the Case

As the heavenly scene unfolds, something subtle becomes clear in which the momentum of this encounter does not belong to the Accuser. God is the one who initiates the exchange. God is the one who frames the conversation. And God is the one who places the question on the table. Satan responds, but he does not lead.

When God asks the Accuser where he has been, Satan answers, "From going to and fro on the earth, and from walking up and down on it." (Job 1:7) At first glance, the statement can sound casual, almost evasive. But in the Hebrew understanding, this language is anything but neutral. It is legal, territorial, and investigative.

To "go to and fro" is the language of patrolling jurisdiction. To "walk up and down" is the language of inspection, and of surveying ground that one believes is vulnerable or contested. This is not idle wandering. It is the posture of an adversary actively searching for weakness, looking for ground to claim, lives to accuse, and devotion to expose as hollow.

Peter later describes the devil as one who prowls, "seeking whom he may devour." (1 Peter 5:8) Zechariah speaks of watchers who patrol the earth, reporting what they find. (Zechariah 1:10-11) In other words, Satan sees himself as a prosecuting attorney moving through his perceived territory as he inspects humanity for cracks in the covenant. And his meaning is implicitly saying, "I have been searching the earth for someone vulnerable."

Then comes the moment that has unsettled readers for centuries. God says, "Have you considered My servant Job?" (Job 1:8)

At first glance, many, including myself, have always wondered, "why on earth would God do that?" But the truth is that this is not an oversight or even recklessness. It is initiative.

God brings Job into the conversation because Satan cannot.

Satan has been patrolling, searching, and inspecting, yet he has not touched Job, accused him, or even named Job. And when God points

Job out, Satan's immediate response is not accusation but admission: "Have You not put a hedge around him?" (Job 1:9)

In a single sentence, the Accuser confesses his own limitation.

The hedge reveals that Job is spiritually protected. He is beyond Satan's reach. And his life, his household, and his integrity stand as a rebuke to the Accuser's claims. Satan cannot penetrate the boundary God has established, and he knows it.

Job 1–2 makes something very clear once we slow down and listen carefully to the language of the courtroom. Satan's accusation is not against Job, it is actually against God.

The question Satan asks is deceptively simple: "Has Job feared God for nothing?" (Job 1:9). But beneath that question lies a sweeping indictment. Satan does not allege hidden sin, or accuse Job of hypocrisy in the conventional sense. Instead, he turns his gaze upward and levels his charge at the throne itself.

The accusation is not, "Job is unrighteous."

The accusation is, "God, You are not worthy of trust."

Satan's logic unfolds with a pointed precision, in that, if Job fears God, it is not because God is intrinsically good. It is because God is profitable. If Job worships, it is not love; it is transactional. And if Job is righteous, it is not transformation; it is self-interest rewarded. In Satan's framework, devotion is never freely given. It is always purchased.

So, his charges stack one upon another:

Job doesn't love You, he loves Your gifts.

Your righteousness cannot actually produce righteousness in anyone.

Your covenant love is not relational; it is transactional.

Remove the blessings, and the worship will collapse into curses.

This is not cynicism about humanity; it is slander against God.

So, at its core, Satan is arguing that God's goodness is ineffective, that His love is manipulative, and that His righteousness cannot create genuine love. According to the Accuser, God does not form worshippers; He manages behavior. And He does not cultivate intimacy; He maintains leverage.

That is why this accusation strikes at the very heart of God's identity. It is an assault on God's character, integrity, covenant, righteousness and His ability to form true worshippers. And it's an attack on God's ability to cultivate relationships with people who love Him for who He is, not for what He gives.

But this accusation is not new. In Genesis 3, the serpent whispers the same lie in a different form through which God's goodness is a lie. He is withholding. He cannot be trusted. Obedience costs more than it gives. The fruit will reveal what God is hiding. So, the question is the same: Is God truly good, or is He protecting His own power?

In Revelation 12, Satan is named explicitly as "the accuser of the brethren," the one who accuses day and night before God. His posture never changes. His strategy never evolves. He is relentless in his attempt to fracture trust between God and humanity by questioning God's character.

Job thus stands directly in the center of this ancient accusation. And this is the crucial reversal the book invites us to see in which Job is not the one on trial. God is.

Job becomes the evidence. His life, his faith, his lament, his refusal to sever relationship even when stripped of everything, all of it unfolds as a living testimony in the cosmic courtroom. So, the question is not whether Job will endure, but whether God's righteousness can produce a human being who loves Him without leverage.

And God is confident in the answer.

Thus, the question many ask, "Why do the righteous suffer?", while valid, may not necessarily be the right question to ask when confronting the book of Job.

It is asking, "Is God righteous?" Is He worthy of trust when blessing is removed? Is His love strong enough to hold a human soul when everything else is gone? Is covenant intimacy real, or is it an illusion sustained by prosperity?

By allowing Job's story to unfold, God willingly places His own character under scrutiny before all of heaven and earth. And Job, though confused, grieving, lamenting, but refusing to let go, becomes the unfolding proof that Satan's accusation is false.

This is why God asks the question. Not as an invitation to destruction, but as a challenge to a worldview. He is pointing to the one human life that already disproves Satan's accusation.

In effect, God is saying, "Your framework cannot explain him."

Because if Satan's theory were true; if devotion were always transactional, if righteousness were merely a product of blessing, then Job should not exist. A man who fears God, loves Him deeply, walks in integrity, and asks nothing in return should be impossible under Satan's assumptions. And yet Job stands there, hedged, whole, and faithful.

The hedge proves several things at once. Satan is limited. God is sovereign. Job belongs to God. And Satan cannot act without permission. Nothing about this scene suggests chaos or risk. Rather, everything about it reveals order, authority, and control.

So, what God is doing here is not exposing Job. He is exposing the lie. More than that, God is willingly placing Himself under scrutiny.

In a single question, God brings His own righteousness, His own covenant love, and His own relational integrity into the open before the entire heavenly host. He allows the Accuser to test the accusation fully, not because God doubts Himself, but because He knows the outcome.

This is why Satan reacts instead of initiates. He does not bring the case; he responds to it. God sets the terms, He defines the evidence, determines the limits, and already knows what Job's life will reveal.

So, God is not testing Job to see what will happen. He is revealing what has already been true. Job's life is not a question mark; it is a witness. And the trial that follows is not about discovering whether God is trustworthy, but about making His trustworthiness visible.

The Accuser believes exposure will collapse devotion, but God knows that exposure will vindicate love.

So, God initiates the case, not to endanger His servant, but to unveil the depth of covenant faith, and in doing so, to place His own character on display before heaven and earth.

Job's Righteousness Vindicates God's Righteousness

Throughout the rest of the story, the reader is brought down from the heights of the heavenly courtroom and placed firmly back on the ash heap with Job himself. The perspective shifts, but the trial does not end. Instead, it begins to unfold in real time on the ground, and within the lived experience of a man who knows nothing of the cosmic proceedings that have just taken place. Job is never informed of the wager. He never hears the accusation. He never receives context. And yet the reader does.

We are given omniscient access while Job is left in the dark. We are allowed to see the heavenly challenge while being forced to feel the human cost. In doing so, the book positions us as witnesses alongside heaven, while simultaneously binding us emotionally to Job's bewildered perspective. We are invited to observe the trial from both angles at once: from God's throne and from the dust of human suffering. Few texts demand this kind of double vision.

And with the terms set, the question presses forward relentlessly.

If Job only worships God when life is good, then the Accuser is right. But if Job continues to love God when blessing is removed...

If he continues to seek God when heaven is silent...

If he continues to cry out rather than walk away...

If he continues to wrestle with God rather than replace Him...

then something far greater is proven. It proves that God is worthy of love apart from His gifts. It proves that God's righteousness can actually produce true righteousness in a human being. And it proves that covenant love is not a contract, but a relationship capable of surviving devastation.

This is where the story turns on its axis. Because Job's perseverance is not, at its core, a test of Job's strength. It is a revelation of God's goodness. Job is not being examined to see how much pain he can endure; God is being revealed as worthy of devotion even when devotion costs everything.

So, every lament and anguished cry is no longer a threat to God's case, it is part of the evidence. And Job's refusal to sever the relationship, even when stripped of explanation, becomes the living contradiction to Satan's accusation. His faith is not polished, but it is real. And that reality vindicates God.

God's silence, then, plays a dual and deliberate role throughout the narrative. On one level, it preserves the integrity of the trial itself. Any direct intervention, explanatory word, or any comforting reassurance would "tamper with the evidence." The question under examination is whether God is worthy of trust without incentive, without explanation, and without immediate reassurance. Therefore, silence is the only environment in which that question can be answered honestly.

But on another level, that same silence becomes formative. It is not merely the backdrop of the trial; it is the crucible in which Job's faith is refined. Everything Job believes about God is tested in the absence of God's response. Every instinct within him cries out to abandon what no longer seems to hold. And yet, in the silence, Job wrestles rather than retreats. And he refuses to replace God with a system, a doctrine, or despair.

In that wrestling, something extraordinary happens. Job's faith matures, deepens, and sheds illusions. It moves from inherited understanding into embodied trust. The silence that seems cruel then becomes the space where covenant faith proves its authenticity.

And so, through the silence, both Job and God are vindicated at the same time. Job is vindicated because his faith is shown to be genuine, relational, and resilient. God is vindicated because His love is shown to be worthy of devotion apart from reward.

The Accuser's charge thus collapses under the weight of this lived reality.

So, in the end, the trial does not conclude with a verdict spoken aloud in heaven. It concludes with a life lived faithfully in the dark. And that life answers the accusation more powerfully than any argument ever could.

NOTES

NOTES

CHAPTER SIX

The Whirlwind, the Revelation, and the Restoration of Job

There is also a common assumption that hangs over the book in which God never truly answers Job's questions. That God avoids the issue, changes the subject, or overwhelms Job with power rather than responding to his pain. But that assumption only holds if we misunderstand what Job has been asking all along.

God does answer Job. And He answers him fully, just not at the level modern readers often expect. God responds at the level from which Job himself has been crying out.

Notice how Job never asks, "Why am I suffering?", "What did I do wrong?", or "Why did You allow this to happen to me?" Those questions are often placed on Job by readers who are uncomfortable sitting in his unresolved pain. But they are not the questions Job actually asks.

Job's cry throughout the entire book is far more intimate. So, if we were to summarize his question into a single plea, it would more accurately be: Where are You? Let me hear You. Let me see You. Do not remain silent.

You see, Job is not seeking a reason, he is seeking God. And this is the thread that runs beneath every lament, protest, and anguished argument. Job does not want a system that explains his suffering. He wants the face of the One he has loved and served. So what he ultimately wants and pleads for throughout the book is God's presence, not answers. This becomes clear to us when we listen carefully to Job's own words.

In Job 13, his desire becomes explicit when he states, "I desire to argue my case with God... Let Him answer me." Notice how Job does not say, "Let Him explain Himself." He wants dialogue and he wants presence. Job wants the sound of God's voice breaking the silence that has become unbearable because information alone will not satisfy him. And Job is not asking God to prove Himself, he is asking that he might plead his own case before God.

In Job 19, his hope moves beyond the present altogether. He says, "I know that my Redeemer lives... and after my skin has been destroyed, yet in my flesh I shall see God." Here, Job's longing is not for vindication alone, it is for resurrection, for union, and for seeing God. His hope is not that his suffering will make sense, but that God Himself will stand with him in the end.

In Job 23, the cry is further stripped down to its simplest form as Job cries, "Oh, that I knew where I might find Him." Again, this is not a demand for explanation, but the ache of absence. Job wants nearness. And he wants to know that the relationship still holds. That God is still there.

Taken together, these passages reveal that Job's real question is not intellectual, but relational. And he is not asking *why*, but *where*. This is why God never explains the reason for Job's suffering. Not because God is evasive or indifferent. But because Job never asked for an explanation. He asked for God. And so, when God finally answers, He gives Job exactly what he has been asking for all along.

Throughout the entire story, the God who had seemed silent finally steps into the whirlwind and speaks. And in doing so, He answers Job at the deepest level possible. Because Job wanted God. And God gave him exactly that and more.

God Answers Through Revelation

Notice when God finally answers Job, that He does not do so quietly or with gentle reasoning. God answers through a glory-storm, and a kind of descent that feels as overwhelming as it is intentional. Because the whirlwind is God's embodied answer to Job's recurrent cry.

And what's most amazing in this is that God's presence alone would have been enough for Job in that moment. After chapters of silence, even a single word would have satisfied Job's longing. But God does more than appear. He speaks. God's subsequent speech is the very revelation through an unveiling of who He is and how reality truly works.

Through His words, God reveals a world far larger than Job's pain, yet is never detached from it. He reveals divine order and untamed wildness existing side by side. This, in itself, is a paradox in which the coexistence of beauty and danger, structure and mystery, sovereignty and freedom can all be contained in one single source. God speaks of His governance over chaos and life alike, of creatures both fearsome and gentle, and of forces humanity cannot control, yet He sustains it all effortlessly. And woven through every image is the same truth that God is intimately involved in all things, not just distantly managing them from afar.

So, these revelations are not distractions from Job's suffering, they are actually the answer. God is not dismissing Job's questions. He is actually answering them at a deeper level than Job knew how to ask. Furthermore, the voice from the whirlwind is not meant to silence Job, it is meant to reorient him.

Even more strikingly, what God reveals in the whirlwind corresponds directly to how the book began. The story opens in a heavenly courtroom, with an accusation leveled against God's righteousness. Then it ends with a final courtroom verdict that is spoken through glory itself.

In the beginning, Satan challenges God's character, questioning whether His righteousness can produce genuine love. And Job becomes the evidence placed under scrutiny. But in the end, God reveals His glory as truth made visible for all to see. And in that revelation, Job is integrated, healed, and restored. His inner fragmentation ends, his striving quiets, his longing is met, and both God and Job are vindicated together.

Notice also, how the themes that God unveils in the whirlwind also mirror the tensions that have defined the entire book: wildness and tameness, order and chaos, good and evil, creaturely limits and spiritual wisdom. God does not resolve these tensions by eliminating one side. Rather, He reveals that He governs both simultaneously. And in doing so, He resolves the trial itself, as the revelation becomes the final verdict.

God also does not explain suffering away. Instead, He reveals Himself within it. And the whirlwind does not answer every question, but it answers the only one that ultimately mattered in whether God is present.

He is also sovereign, good, and is indeed worthy of trust, even when the world remains wild.

And Job, having finally encountered the living God he refused to let go of, finds that presence is indeed enough.

God Honors Job's Embittered Cry

As we progress through the book, most readers can instinctively recoil from Job's tone. His words sound sharp, even dangerous at times. And his accusations seem to cross lines we have been taught not to cross. By conventional religious standards, Job appears irreverent in which he is too bold, too raw, and too unrestrained. Yet, when God finally speaks, He does not rebuke Job for his tone. He honors him.

This alone often leaves readers baffled.

As we previously discussed, God honors Job because his posture was honest. Job refuses to settle for formulaic answers, and he will not accept inherited explanations that shrink God to manageable proportions. He rejects not only the reasoning of his friends, but even his own limited attempts to make sense of the disaster. Again and again, Job pushes past human frameworks and demands God Himself.

Because what Job wants is not explanations crafted by human logic, he longs most deeply for relational presence. This is why Job does not side with human understanding, and not even his own. He knows that every system collapses under the weight of real suffering. And so, he refuses to anchor himself in what can be understood. Instead, he anchors himself in the One who cannot be reduced.

God's Answer Brings Psychological and Spiritual Integration

Furthermore, when God speaks, something amazing happens within Job. Fear begins to loosen its grip. Confusion no longer dominates his inner world. And the fragmented voices that have been battling inside him all fall silent as they are rendered meaningless in the presence of truth. And this is the moment that Job becomes whole.

For chapters, Job has been divided as he was pulled between tradition and fear, condemnation and hope, longing and confusion. Each voice demanded allegiance, and offered only a partial explanation that ultimately failed. But when spiritual reality meets the human soul directly, fragmentation cannot survive. So, God does not argue with Job's inner divisions, He integrates them.

This is the moment when the human psyche encounters such a reality without mediation, distortion, or defense. Job no longer needs to resolve the tension between what he believes, and what he feels or needs to choose between reverence and honesty. Because in God's presence, those false oppositions collapse.

So, what now emerges is a person no longer divided against himself. His soul has become unified as he stands before the One who holds everything together. And his cry is never corrected but fulfilled. And God does not shame Job for his embittered honesty. Instead, He meets it fully. And in so doing, He brings a fractured soul back into wholeness through presence, revelation, and through intimacy restored.

God Incorporates Job into the Resolution

But God does not stop at appearing. He does not stop at revealing Himself. And He does not stop at restoring Job's inner world. What God does next in chapter 42 is astonishing.

After vindicating Job, exposing the insufficiency of the friends' theology, and integrating Job's fractured soul through revelation, God draws Job directly into the resolution of the entire matter. He does not merely end the trial; He completes it through participation.

God turns to Job and says, in effect, "Intercede for your friends." In this moment, God publicly appoints Job—the very man who was misjudged, accused, and spiritually dissected—as the one who will now stand between heaven and those who wounded him. So, Job is no longer simply the suffering righteous man, he is now commissioned.

In this act, God establishes Job as an intercessor, a priest, a mediator, and a restorer. This is not punishment disguised as humility. Nor is it God forcing Job into reluctant forgiveness. Rather, God is entrusting Job with priestly authority at the very moment his righteousness is vindicated. So, the one who was falsely accused and endured the silence is now entrusted with reconciliation through God's redemptive work.

And notice the order: Job is not asked to intercede *instead* of being vindicated, but *because* he has been. His suffering is not minimized; it is honored. His lament is not corrected; it is fulfilled. And now, his restored intimacy with God becomes the means through which others are restored as well.

And having passed through suffering into restored intimacy, he is raised, not merely to relief, but to intercession. So, this pattern reveals that suffering leads not only to restoration, but to priesthood. In this way, Job does not merely survive the trial, he becomes part of its resolution.

It's important to note, however, that the book does not end with Job proven right and the friends proven wrong. It ends with reconciliation mediated through the very one who suffered. God could have forgiven the friends directly. He could have dismissed their errors without ceremony. But instead, He chooses to heal the fracture through Job's intercession. Why? Because God is not only interested in correcting theology. He is interested in restoring relationships.

Job's role as mediator reveals the deepest logic of the book in which suffering, when met with covenant faithfulness, does not terminate in isolation, it expands into redemptive authority. Job's pain thus becomes the soil from which priestly compassion grows. And his restored intimacy with God becomes the channel through which others are brought back into right standing.

Thus, Job is not simply the subject of the story. He becomes a reflection of the greater Man of Sorrows. His life points forward to the One who would suffer innocently, be vindicated by God, and rise to intercede for those who misunderstood and condemned Him.

In the end, Job is not only healed, he is restored and incorporated into God's redemptive purpose. So, in this final act, the book of Job reveals that God does not only answer suffering, He redeems it by drawing the faithful sufferer into the work of reconciliation itself.

NOTES

NOTES

CHAPTER SEVEN

The Righteous Sufferer and the Foreshadowing of the Gospel

As we have touched on in earlier chapters, the book of Job calls to a pattern that reaches forward beyond Job himself and gestures most certainly toward Christ. Job becomes a reflective image that reveals the shape of the gospel long before it arrives in fullness.

Before the trial begins, or even before any accusation is ever raised, God Himself speaks. And what God declares is a public statement of approval. He names Job's character before the entire host of heaven saying, "Have you considered My servant Job? ...There is none like him on the earth." (Job 1:8)

This declaration is foundational to the entire story because Job's righteousness is not inferred by human observation, but is pronounced by God Himself. It is recognized, affirmed, and publicly declared in the highest court of heaven before any suffering ever unfolds. In other words, Job is not later discovered to be righteous through endurance, he is righteous before the trial ever begins.

But this pattern is not unique to Job. Abraham is declared righteous by faith before the covenant reaches its fullness. And Jesus, standing at the Jordan river, hears the voice of the Father declare, "This is My beloved Son," (Matthew 3:17) before His public ministry begins and before His suffering unfolds. In each case, righteousness is named prior to trial, and identity precedes testing.

So Job's suffering does not arise from hidden sin, moral failure, or God's displeasure. It arises precisely because he is righteous. Like Christ, Job suffers not because he is guilty, but because he is faithful. And this is why the book cannot end without vindication for not only Job, but for God Himself. To leave righteousness crushed and unanswered would be to validate the Accuser's claim.

Yet even as Job stands as a righteous sufferer, the text is careful not to blur the distinction between shadow and substance in which Job is righteous, but he is not *the* Righteous One. Job is chosen, blameless, and upright. Yet, Job is not capable of bearing the full weight of righteousness. And though Job is blameless and righteous, he is not sinless or perfect. Therefore, he is unable to stand unshielded beneath divine scrutiny.

This is the essence of Old Covenant righteousness. It is genuine, relational, and God-honoring, but it cannot finally reconcile the human soul to God without mediation, and Job knows this.

As the trial progresses and the silence deepens, Job reaches a breaking point of self-reliance. The more honestly he examines himself, the clearer it becomes that even his righteousness cannot save him. And that even if he were brought into God's presence to plead his case, he realizes that his own lips would condemn him as he confesses in Job 9.

You see, Job recognizes that his righteousness, as noble as it is, cannot bridge the chasm between Creator and creature. And it is in this place that Job's longing arises; not for vindication alone, but for mediation.

Job cries out for someone who can lay a hand on both God and man. Someone who can stand without collapsing, and whose righteousness is not merely declared, but inherent. This is the Old Testament soul discovering the necessity of Christ.

So, Job's story does not diminish righteousness, but exposes its limits. And in doing so, it prepares the ground for the gospel itself. Job stands as the righteous sufferer who cannot save himself, pointing forward to the Righteous One who can. His suffering reveals the need for a mediator not yet revealed, but already anticipated in Jesus Christ.

And it is here that Job's plea for a mediator is not merely a moment of emotional desperation, but a picture of the gospel embedded in the heart of the Old Testament. When Job cries out for someone who can lay a hand on both God and man, he is articulating something no covenant, sacrifice, or system has yet been able to provide as he is reaching beyond the categories available to him and naming a need that only Christ can fulfill.

Job longs for one who can stand between heaven and earth without being consumed by either. Someone who can plead his case without distorting God's justice. And Someone who can reconcile him to God without denying the reality of his suffering. Job is not asking for vindication through an argument, but asking for reconciliation through a person.

Yet this is not an abstract hope for Job as he says, "I know that my Redeemer lives." (Job 19:25) That statement alone is the reorientation of his hope. And it is here that Job's confidence shifts away from his own righteousness, away from his ability to defend himself, and away from the fragile structures that once gave his life meaning. His hope becomes anchored in Someone he has not yet seen, but whom he knows must exist.

Up to this point, Job has been striving to understand, to defend himself, and to reconcile his experience with what he knows of God. And he has argued relentlessly because he refuses to let go of that relationship. But here, something changes, and the striving gives way to surrender. The arguments give way to longing, and the focus shifts from the self to the Redeemer.

So, Job's longing becomes the spiritual doorway through which revelation will eventually enter. Before God ever speaks from the whirlwind, Job has already moved from demanding answers to desiring a Savior. His heart has been stripped of every illusion of self-sufficiency, and in that stripped-down place, the gospel takes shape in seed form.

Job does not yet know the name of Jesus. Nor has he yet seen the cross. But he knows that he cannot save himself, and God must provide the bridge. And it is precisely this longing that prepares Job to recognize the true magnitude of God when He finally speaks.

In this way, Job's cry does more than express suffering, it prophesies redemption. It reaches forward through time, carrying the ache of every righteous sufferer who will come after him, until it finds its answer in the One who truly can lay a hand on both God and man. And that One is Jesus Himself.

Job's story shows us what righteous suffering looks like in a fallen world. He gives language to our ache and gives shape to the longing. He shows us what it means to suffer without letting go of God.

But Christ fulfills what Job could only foreshadow. Christ does not merely endure righteous suffering, He conquers it. And He does not only remain faithful under it; He transforms it into redemption. In other words, Job's story prepares the soil that Christ fully brings into harvest.

The Descent into Ashes and Christ's Resurrection

Job's descent into the ashes in chapter 2 also portrays a scene that is both humiliating and heartbreaking. Once clothed in honor, he now sits on the ground, scraping his sores with broken pottery, surrounded by what remains of his former life. The ashes in this picture are symbolic of the visible confession of mortality, grief, repentance, and the limits of even the most upright human righteousness. Ashes are what remain when everything else has been burned away.

In the ancient world, to sit in ashes was to acknowledge the truth no argument can escape in which you are dust, and to dust you will return. Job does not merely suffer emotionally or spiritually; he is brought face-to-face with the finality of humanity itself. His body fails, his understanding collapses, and his righteousness, though real and sincere, cannot lift him out of the dust. It is here, at the lowest point imaginable, that Job's story becomes most honest because human righteousness, no matter how blameless, always ends in ashes. It cannot resurrect itself or transcend death. It can only testify to its own limits.

And Job stays there until God ultimately intervenes.

But Jesus does not merely sit among the ashes of human suffering; He enters death itself. So, where Job tastes mortality, Christ swallows it whole. And where Job is reduced to dust, Christ descends into the grave. But unlike Job, Christ does not remain there. Christ's resurrection marks the beginning of something entirely new. It is not the restoration of the old order, but the inauguration of new creation. And what Job's ashes testify to through human insufficiency, Christ's resurrection answers with His own sufficiency.

His rising announces that what humanity could not lift from the dust, God Himself has raised in glory. Job shows us where the road ends if righteousness depends on man. But Christ shows us where it truly begins when righteousness is given by God.

God Prevents Job From Being Destroyed

Yet while Job suffers profoundly, he is never handed over completely to destruction. God Himself establishes the boundaries of the trial before it ever begins.

When Satan challenges God regarding Job's devotion, God permits testing, but only within strict limits as Satan is not given free rein. He is restrained and governed.

First, God allows Satan to touch Job's possessions, but not Job himself. Later, Satan is permitted to afflict Job's body, but God draws a hard boundary as He says, "Spare his life." (Job 2:6) This establishes a jurisdiction in which Satan may test, but he may not destroy Job.

And it also reveals something essential about the nature of the trial in which Job is never in Satan's hands because he remains in God's. While the suffering Job experiences is real, devastating, and overwhelming, it is not annihilating. God does not abandon Job to chaos, He governs the chaos. The hedge is partially lowered, but not removed. And Satan can wound Job, but he cannot consume him.

This restraint is mercy, and it mirrors a consistent biblical pattern throughout Scripture. When Isaac is bound on Mount Moriah, the knife never falls. God halts the sacrifice before death occurs and intervenes with a substitute. (Genesis 22:9-13) The obedience is proven without requiring destruction.

Likewise, the scapegoat ritual acknowledges sin and judgment, but diverts death away from the people in which judgment is real, but it is restrained, and life is preserved. (Leviticus 16)

Job stands within this same pattern in which he is righteous, but he is not appointed for destruction. He is appointed for witness. In other words, his role is not to bear judgment fully, but to expose the lie that righteousness only exists for reward. And because that is his role, God ensures from the outset that Job will not be crushed beyond recovery.

Job is righteous, but he is not the Lamb.

Only Christ will be handed over without restraint. Only Christ will face judgment without limits. And only Christ will be allowed to descend fully into death and rise again. So, where Job's suffering is bounded by mercy, Christ's suffering is unbounded for the sake of redemption. Job is protected because his substitution is coming.

God prevents Job from being destroyed because the full weight of accusation, judgment, and death must fall elsewhere. The righteous sufferer of Job points forward to the Righteous One who will not be spared. Job's life is preserved precisely because he is not the final answer.

So, from the very beginning, the book of Job quietly testifies to this truth that suffering may be permitted, but destruction belongs only to the cross. And Job's story is held within mercy while Christ's story will carry judgment to its end.

The wisdom of Job, therefore, prepares the heart to recognize the gospel when it arrives. It teaches us that human righteousness cannot rescue itself, that suffering demands more than explanation, and that only God Himself can bridge the distance between heaven and earth. Job's cry reaches forward into history, and Christ answers it fully.

So, this book tells us the truth about humanity, while the resurrection tells us the truth about God. And between them stands the gospel, where the righteous sufferer is no longer spared, but given, so that suffering itself might finally be redeemed.

NOTES

NOTES

CHAPTER EIGHT

Sanctification Through Suffering

There is another question that continues to surface as the story moves forward, and it is one that quietly lingers beneath the narrative for the reader. But it is not a question that can be dismissed or explained away without first wrestling honestly with all that has already preceded it. Because the truth is, suffering exists in this world regardless of where one stands on God's sovereignty, human agency, or any perceived lack thereof. The world suffers. Creation groans. And that reality does not change based on our theological frameworks.

So the question remains: why is there even a need for suffering at all? And more specifically, why must believers suffer?

Yes, the world is broken and longing for restoration. That much is clear. Yet Scripture goes further and tells us that those who pursue righteousness are not merely affected by suffering, but are often called directly into it.

Why?

Worldviews may shape how we talk about suffering, but they do not remove it. And debate may refine language, but it does not silence the groaning of creation itself. That groaning precedes our conclusions and outlasts any of our arguments. So the real question is not whether suffering exists, but why it remains necessary, especially for those who belong to God.

But Scripture never treats suffering as a problem to be solved before it treats it as a reality to be faced. And its answer is uncomfortable for us because it cannot be reduced to punishment, accident, or God's indifference.

From the beginning, righteousness in a fallen world is confrontational by nature. So, to live aligned with God's character is to live out of step with a world ordered by fear, power, self-preservation, and death. That very misalignment produces friction. And that friction produces suffering, not as an arbitrary test, but as the inevitable consequence of truth entering a hostile terrain.

This is why Scripture consistently frames suffering for believers as participation rather than punishment (Romans 8:17; 1 Peter 4:13). Righteousness exposes what is false. And when righteousness enters a broken world, it destabilizes systems built on illusion, control, and self-justification. That destabilization provokes resistance.

Job does not suffer because he is guilty, but because his righteousness dismantles the Accuser's claim (Job 1:8–11; Job 2:3–5). The prophets suffer not because they are wrong, but because truth threatens false security (Jeremiah 20:7–9; 2 Chronicles 24:20–21). And Christ does not suffer because He failed, but because perfect righteousness cannot coexist peacefully with a world enslaved to sin and death (John 1:11; John 15:24–25). So, suffering is not the goal, it is the cost of fidelity in a fractured creation (1 Peter 2:19–23).

But then, another question naturally follows: why doesn't God simply remove suffering now?

Because redemption is not accomplished by bypassing reality, but by entering it and transforming it from within (John 1:14; Hebrews 2:14–18).

If God removed suffering without addressing the deeper disease, He would be managing symptoms rather than healing creation. But Scripture reveals that God's method of restoration is enacted by entering the brokenness, bearing its weight, and redeeming it from the inside out.

This is why suffering becomes formative for believers. Not because pain is holy, but because true trust is revealed under pressure. Love is clarified when reward disappears, and faith becomes real when it no longer depends on the outcomes.

And believers are not merely recipients of salvation, but are participants in restoration. To suffer with Christ is not to add to His work, but to be shaped by it. This is how the old self loosens its grip and how illusions die. It is also how intimacy deepens as suffering strips away the false gods that comfort would otherwise leave untouched.

Scripture never promises a suffering-free life (John 16:33; Acts 14:22). But it does promise meaning, presence, and transformation within suffering (2 Corinthians 4:16–18; Romans 5:3–5).

This is the deeper answer the book of Job leads us toward, as it reveals what suffering is capable of producing when it is met with faith. In suffering, the true character of God is revealed just as the foundations of faith are exposed. And a people are formed who trust God even when the world remains unresolved (Romans 5:3–5). This is sanctification at work.

Sanctification refines the soul into deeper likeness with God (Romans 8:29). And Scripture repeatedly affirms that suffering, when borne in faith, becomes the means by which God shapes His people. Jesus is the ultimate righteous sufferer. And believers, united to Christ, become sanctified sufferers because God meets His people within it.

This is why the New Testament sounds so much like Job.

James urges believers to count it joy when they encounter trials, not because pain is good, but because testing produces perseverance, and perseverance completes its work (James 1:2–4). Peter tells believers not to be surprised by fiery trials, but to rejoice insofar as they share in Christ's sufferings (1 Peter 4:12–13). Paul speaks of suffering producing endurance, character, and hope (Romans 5:3–4), and confesses his longing to know Christ not only in power, but in the fellowship of His sufferings (Philippians 3:10).

Righteousness leads into suffering. Suffering tests faithfulness. And faithfulness is ultimately vindicated by God (Job 42:7–10; Romans 8:18). This is the pattern of sanctification itself.

Suffering also strips away the old self (Ephesians 4:22–24; Colossians 3:9–10). Romans speaks of conformity to Christ's image (Romans 8:29). Peter speaks of faith refined by fire (1 Peter 1:6–7). Hebrews speaks of discipline that produces holiness (Hebrews 12:10–11). James speaks of perseverance completing its work (James 1:4). And Philippians speaks of knowing Christ through suffering (Philippians 3:10).

It is a fire that does not destroy, but purifies. Because suffering reveals what cannot otherwise be seen. It exposes the heart, reveals the depth of intimacy with God, and uncovers the battle between hardening and yielding. It tests whether trust is rooted in outcomes or in God Himself.

And the truth of the matter is that suffering is never neutral. It is either formative or deformative, depending on how the heart responds.

Every figure shaped by God passes through a wilderness before stepping into fullness: Israel (Deuteronomy 8:2–3), David (1 Samuel 22:1–2; Psalm 63:1), Elijah (1 Kings 19:4–8), Jesus (Matthew 4:1–11), Paul (Galatians 1:17), and Job in the ashes (Job 2:8).

The setting may change, but the purpose does not. The wilderness is always where intimacy is forged, identity is revealed, and a believer's calling is refined. Suffering presses the soul with a single unavoidable question that asks us how we will endure it.

Will you love God for God alone? (Job 1:9–11)

Will you trust when there is no answer? (Job 23:8–10)

Will you worship in the ashes? (Job 2:9–10)

Will you meet God in the whirlwind rather than fleeing from it? (Job 38:1; Job 42:5)

Ultimately, Job's suffering is meant to serve as a revelation for the reader who studies it. And through it, we are shown that the God who allows suffering is the same God who uses it, not to distance His people, but to draw them closer than they have ever been before.

NOTES

NOTES

CHAPTER NINE

The God Who Has Always Been Vindicated

From the beginning of creation, God's character has stood under scrutiny. The first accusation did not question human obedience; it questioned God's goodness. Did God really say? Can He be trusted? Is His Word true, or is His authority self-serving? From Eden forward, the accusation has remained remarkably consistent, even as history unfolded and generations changed.

The book of Job pulls back the veil and shows us that this scrutiny was never merely earthly. God's righteousness, His covenant love, His faithfulness, and His ability to form true worshippers were placed before the heavenly host. And yet, in every generation, in every covenant, and in every unfolding act of redemption, God has remained the same. He has not adjusted His character to survive accusation. He has not revised His Word to defend Himself. Nor has He compromised His promises to silence doubt. He has simply remained faithful.

Job's story sits within that larger testimony as the trial was not ultimately resolved by explanation or argument. It was resolved by consistency. God remained who He had always been, even when His silence was misunderstood. Job remained faithful not because suffering made sense, but because God's character had already proven itself trustworthy. And in that relationship, God's righteousness stood vindicated without a single word needing to be spoken in its defense.

That same question continues to surface in our own time, today, but the answer has not changed, because God has not changed. God has not vindicated Himself through power displays alone, nor through the removal of suffering, nor through philosophical clarity. He has vindicated Himself through love, with His own faithfulness, and ultimately, He has answered it through the Cross.

At Calvary, God placed His own heart on public display. The Cross stands as the final and irreversible vindication of God's character. It declares that His love is not transactional, His righteousness is not self-serving, and His covenant faithfulness is not fragile. God did not preserve Himself from suffering to prove His goodness; He entered into it completely. And He did not demand trust from a distance. Instead, He bore betrayal, abandonment, and death itself to secure it.

In Christ, the question of God's trustworthiness is no longer theoretical. It is written in His blood. The God who stood accused since Eden stood exposed on the Cross, and remained faithful. And in the resurrection, God's Word, His promises, and His character were sealed forever.

So even though the book of Job does not end with the answers many might expect, it does end with assurance, because the God who was questioned has been revealed. The God who was scrutinized has been vindicated. And the God who remained silent for a season has spoken definitively through His Son.

NOTES

NOTES

AFTERWORD

Job may not have known it, but in his affliction, he was embodying the mystery of the cross. Paul said that there were mysteries hidden for ages, now revealed through Christ (Colossians 1:26). And God doesn't reveal those things to the most qualified, He reveals them to the willing.

You don't need a degree to hear Him. Only hunger. Job had that hunger. And it drew him into a kind of intimacy with God that survived the silence, outlasted the agony, and bore the weight of what he could not explain.

"Search the Scriptures," Jesus said, "for they testify of Me." (John 5:39)

This is the kind of invitation that draws in the soul that longs for the intimacy stripped of all pretense and illusion. And it's the kind of invitation that tells of a story written specifically for you and for me.

The Lamb was slain before the foundation of the world. (Revelation 13:8)

That's the story that God tells. And it's the kind of story Job was a part of, whether he knew it or not.

My hope is that, by looking again at Job through this lens, you'll begin to see the image of Jesus woven through every part of it, and waiting just beneath the surface, ready to be revealed to the one willing to pause and seek.

The beauty of Jesus is that He lays claim to every paradox of our existence. He is the first and the last, the beginning and the end. He is the lion and the lamb. He is the seed, the tree, and the fruit. He is the one who plants, the one who waters, and the one who cultivates growth. He is the living water, the bread of life, and the very breath in our lungs.

And this same Jesus is the one Job longed for; the One he somehow knew he would one day see, even after death, in the flesh (Job 19:25–27). That kind of knowing doesn't come from intellect alone. It comes from intimacy.

God says His mysteries are hidden, not from us, but for us. They are simple enough for a child to receive, and complex enough for a scholar to search out, if they're willing to see with the faith of a child. But all of them lead to Christ.

If you pursue Him as Job did, then you will find what Job found: a God who is not far off. A Judge who defends you. A Redeemer who has already spoken on your behalf.

And that is an assurance and a wisdom that no man can take from you.

SCRIPTURE REFERENCES BY CHAPTER

All passages quoted or referenced are from the Modern English Version

CHAPTER ONE

- Job 1:6–12 — The heavenly council scene where Satan challenges Job's righteousness before God.
- Job 2:1–6 — Satan is permitted to afflict Job further, but only within boundaries set by God.
- Zechariah 3:1–2 — A vision of Satan accusing the high priest, with God rebuking the Accuser.

CHAPTER TWO

- Job 1:8–11 — God declares Job righteous; Satan claims righteousness exists only for reward.
- Job 2:3–5 — Satan intensifies his accusation, arguing that suffering will break Job's faith.
- Genesis 1:31 — God declares creation "very good," establishing His original intent and goodness.
- Genesis 3:1 — The serpent introduces doubt about God's word and character in Eden.

CHAPTER THREE

- Job 3:1–26 — Job laments his existence, expressing grief without denying God.

- Job 13:3 — Job longs to speak directly with God rather than argue with human voices.

- Job 23:3–6 — Job searches for God in His silence, believing God would listen if found.

CHAPTER FOUR

- Job 4:7–8 — Eliphaz asserts that suffering must be the result of sin.

- Job 8:3–7 — Bildad defends God's justice through rigid moral formulas.

- Job 11:4–6 — Zophar insists Job deserves greater punishment than he has received.

CHAPTER FIVE

- Job 9:2–3 — Job acknowledges God's greatness while questioning how any human could answer Him.

- Job 9:28–31 — Job recognizes the inadequacy of his own righteousness before God.

- Job 12:13 — Job affirms that wisdom and power belong to God alone.

CHAPTER SIX

- Job 9:32–33 — Job expresses the need for a mediator between God and humanity.

- Job 16:19–21 — Job declares that his witness is in heaven and pleads for intercession.

- Job 19:25–27 — Job proclaims his hope in a living Redeemer beyond death.

CHAPTER SEVEN

- Job 1:8 — God publicly affirms Job's righteousness before the heavenly court.
- Job 2:8–10 — Job suffers physically yet refuses to curse God.
- Job 9:20 — Job admits that even his own words would condemn him before God.
- Job 19:25 — Job's declaration of hope in a Redeemer.
- Matthew 3:17 — The Father declares Jesus as His beloved Son before His suffering begins.
- Matthew 27:46 — Jesus cries out in perceived abandonment on the cross.
- Hebrews 4:15 — Christ is described as a sympathetic High Priest who suffered without sin.
- Hebrews 12:2 — Jesus endures the cross for the joy set before Him.

CHAPTER EIGHT

- Job 1:9–11 — Satan argues that devotion exists only because of blessing.
- Job 2:9–10 — Job chooses faith over bitterness amid suffering.
- Job 23:8–10 — Job trusts that God is refining him though unseen.
- Job 38:1 — God finally speaks from the whirlwind.
- Job 42:5 — Job moves from secondhand knowledge of God to direct encounter.
- Romans 5:3–5 — Suffering produces endurance, character, and hope.

- Romans 8:17–18 — Believers share in suffering with Christ before sharing in glory.
- Romans 8:29 — God conforms believers to the image of His Son.
- 1 Peter 1:6–7 — Faith is refined through trials like gold in fire.
- 1 Peter 4:12–13 — Believers are called to rejoice in sharing Christ's sufferings.
- James 1:2–4 — Trials produce perseverance that matures faith.
- Hebrews 12:10–11 — God disciplines His children for holiness.
- Philippians 3:10 — Paul desires to know Christ through both power and suffering.
- 2 Corinthians 4:16–18 — Present suffering prepares eternal glory.
- John 16:33 — Jesus promises peace amid tribulation.
- Acts 14:22 — Entry into God's kingdom involves many hardships.

CHAPTER NINE

- Genesis 3:1 — The first accusation against God's trustworthiness.
- Job 42:7–10 — God vindicates Job and restores him.
- John 5:39 — Jesus declares that Scripture testifies about Him.
- John 1:14 — God enters human suffering through the incarnation.
- Hebrews 2:14–18 — Christ shares fully in humanity to defeat death.
- Colossians 1:26 — God reveals mysteries once hidden through Christ.
- Revelation 13:8 — The Lamb was slain before the foundation of the world.

ABOUT THE AUTHOR

Tabitha Min has always believed that stories, whether spoken or written, carry a wonder all their own, one that stays with the reader long after the final page is turned.

She lives in rural South Carolina with her husband and their children. When she's not caring for her family or tending to the home, Tabitha is often working on her next project, reading, or outlining new ideas for the stories ahead.

But her journey is far from over. To discover more about her work, her creations, and the stories yet to come, visit:

www.tabithamin.com

OTHER WORKS BY TABITHA MIN

ESTHER AND THE COVENANT WAR (2025)

The story of Esther is more than a tale of courage within a Persian court—it is a battleground in the ongoing covenant war between God's promise and the powers that seek to oppose it.

Esther and the Covenant War invites readers to trace that ancient conflict from Eden's first promise of redemption, through Esther's stand for her people, to its fulfillment at the Cross of Christ. This expository study reveals how the same spiritual struggle that began in Genesis reverberates through Esther's story and continues to unfold in our own time.

Designed for those who hunger for depth, this study weaves together historical insight, scriptural exposition, and spiritual reflection. It unveils how God's hidden hand transforms human intent into heavenly purpose, and how faith, obedience, and intercession still move the course of kingdoms.

Step into the covenant story that stretches from creation to the cross, and discover how one woman's obedience became a reflection of God's ultimate triumph.

HARU'S WORLD
CHILDREN'S BOOK (2024)

Haru, a little toadstool mush-room, comes to life when a sprinkle of magical dust falls from an ancient oak tree. Awakened to a world of wonder, Haru embarks on a journey of discovery, seeing everything through new eyes and making delightful friends along the way.

FENNEL'S LIGHT
CHILDREN'S BOOK (2025)

When Fennel, a small and unassuming creature, receives an ordinary candle from a wandering traveler, he thinks little of it—until he lights the wick and glimpses a distant glow on the horizon. Compelled by a force he cannot explain, Fennel leaves behind the only home he's ever known to follow the light.

Guided by the flickering glow, Fennel's journey is not without struggle. He faces temptation, deception, and a darkness that seeks to snuff out his flame. But through every trial, the light remains, beckoning him onward. An allegorical fantasy tale reminiscent of Pilgrim's Progress, Fennel's Light is a stirring fable about perseverance, trust, and the faith to walk forward even when the path is uncertain.

DAWN OF AVARICE
BOOK ONE (2023)

Ludica, king of Faermire, has devoted years to building a powerful legacy for his three children. But when the sudden death of a rival king stirs whispers of conflict across the land, Ludica realizes that threats to his reign are closer than he imagined—both beyond his borders and within them.

As Gwenora, the widowed queen, offers Ludica a treaty to secure peace, they both recognize that such an alliance risk inciting rebellion among their own people.

Meanwhile, Ludica's eldest children, Beowyn and Estrith, uncover a plot involving their uncle and stepmother, aimed at seizing the throne. Yet, in bringing the truth to light, they face consequences that threaten to unravel the world around them.

With treasonous alliances, deadly conspiracies, and fractured loyalties at every turn, Ludica and his family must rely on each other to hold their places in the kingdom of Aecorath—or risk losing everything they hold dear.

Scan the QR code to step beyond the page and immerse yourself in the animated audiobook of *Dawn of Avarice*. Watch the story unfold with captivating narration, rich sound design, and stunning visuals that bring the world of Aecorath to life.

PERDITION RISING

BOOK TWO (2025)

The realm teeters on the edge of chaos, and those who remain must navigate treachery, war, and forces beyond mortal under-standing.

Beowyn never sought the crown, but with the throne thrust upon him, he must prove his worth, or risk losing everything. His sister, Estrith, will stop at nothing to save their brother, Siged, from a dark affliction—one that threatens not only his life but the very fabric of their king-dom.

Meanwhile, Sidonis, bound to a fate he does not fully comprehend, walks a dangerous path between ambition and the will of the gods.

Old enemies rise, new alliances take shape, and unseen forces stir beneath the surface. As Aecorath descends further into conflict, those at the center of it all must decide how much they are willing to sacrifice—for power, for loyalty, and for survival.

The gods are watching. The war has only begun.

Stay up to date with the latest projects, upcoming releases, and handcrafted creations. Whether it's new additions to the Siege of Aecorath series, exclusive artwork, or unique, story-inspired items from The Curious Emporium, there is always some-thing new on the horizon.

Explore current works, discover what's to come, and be the first to know about future adventures. Join the journey and step into a world where stories take shape beyond the page.

Books are available for purchase directly through the website or can be found on Amazon.com.

Visit to learn more

www.tabithamin.com

www.ingramcontent.com/pod-product-compliance
Lightning Source LLC
Chambersburg PA
CBHW060631130626
46555CB00002B/747